BOOK TWO OF THE *BELIEVING AN*...

The stone fidelity

BELIEVE TO LIVE

They hardly meant has come to be

ANN WALSH

Their final blazon, and to prove

Our almost-instinct almost true;

VERITAS

What will survive of us is love.

Philip Larkin

First published 1995 by
Veritas Publications
7-8 Lower Abbey Street
Dublin 1

Imprimatur
✠ Desmond Connell
Archbishop of Dublin

Copyright © Veritas Publications 1995

ISBN 1 85390 288 8

The author gratefully acknowledges the work of the Education Sub-Committee of the Episcopal Commission on Catechetics, chaired by Bishop Donal Murray, the contribution of the Post-Primary Diocesan Advisors, and the participation of the teachers who piloted this text.

Design: Bill Bolger
Origination: The Kulor Centre Ltd, Dublin
Printed in the Republic of Ireland by
Smurfit Web Press Ltd

Acknowledgements
Bantam, Doubleday, Dell, *Creative Ministry and Intimacy,* Henri Nouwen; HarperCollins San Francisco, *After Ideology,* David Walsh; Hodder & Stoughton, *Man's Search for Meaning,* Viktor Frankl; Maxwell Macmillan/Collier, *Passion: An Essay on Personality,* Roberto Mangabeira Unger; Darton Longman & Todd Ltd, *Rediscovering Pastoral Care,* Alastair Campbell, *Proposals for a New Sexual Ethic,* Jack Dominian, *Free to Believe,* Michael Paul Gallagher; Rowan Tree Press, *A Book of Sibyls,* Margherita Guidacci; SPCK, *Understanding Veritatis Splendor,* ed. John Williams; *The Irish Times,* article by Paul Smyth; St Mary's Press, *Understanding Catholic Christianity,* Thomas Zanzig; Pádraig Daly, 'Sagart 3'; Twenty-Third Publications, Mystic, CT, *Redemptive Intimacy: A New Perspective for the Journey to Adult Faith,* copyright © 1981 by Dick Westley; Gill & Macmillan, *Has Sin Changed?,* Seán Fagan, *Church, State, Morality and Law,* Patrick Hannon; Ignatius Press, *Introduction to Christianity,* Joseph Ratzinger; Penguin Books Ltd, 'Antigone', from *The Theban Plays* by Sophocles, translated by E. F. Watling (Penguin Classics, 1947) copyright © E. F. Watling, 1947; *A Man for All Seasons* is copyright © Robert Bolt 1966. All rights reserved; New Island Books, *The Road to Silence,* Sean Dunne; Arrow Books, *The Different Drum,* M. Scott Peck; *The Furrow,* Liam Ryan, January 1983 *Furrow,* Vol. 34, no. 1; Bloodaxe Books, 'A Marriage', R. S. Thomas, reprinted by Bloodaxe Books from *Mass for Hard Times* by R. S. Thomas; Burns & Oates Ltd, *Introduction to Christian Faith,* Walter Kasper; Faber & Faber Ltd, *Collected Poems 1909-1962* and *Murder in the Cathedral,* T. S. Eliot, *Collected Poems,* Philip Larkin, *Lord of the Flies,* William Golding; extracts from *The Christian Heritage,* Desmond Forristal, *Life in All its Fullness,* Donal Murray, *Irish Catholics,* John J. Ó Ríordáin, *Can These Bones Live?,* Donal Murray, *The Church – Guardian of Freedom,* Donal Murray, *Handing on the Faith in the Home, The Moral Life,* and *Love is for Life* are published by Veritas Publications; the English translation of the *Catechism of the Catholic Church* (for Ireland) is copyright © 1994 Veritas-Libreria Editrice Vaticana. All rights reserved; the text of the Marriage Rite is copyright © 1970, 1980, the Catholic Communications Institute of Ireland Inc. All rights reserved.

Illustrations
pp. 4, 31, 117, © Alain Pinoges/CIRIC; pp. 19, 114, CIRIC; pp. 8, 10, 19, 60, 64, 74, Mary Evans Picture Library; p. 15, National Museum of Ireland; pp. 28, 75, 90, Bill Bolger; pp. 48, 98, Luke Golobitsh; p. 55, © Anaïk Frantz/CIRIC; p. 57, © G. Giuliani/CIRIC; p. 69, SCALA; p. 76, National Portrait Gallery; p. 85, Mary Evans/Sigmund Frued Copyrights; p. 93 Bord Fáilte; p. 97 © Michael Gauvry/CIRIC; p. 102, Judges of Hastings. The front cover illustration is a carved panel depicting Adam and Eve under the Tree of Life, Ardmore Church. Reproduced with the permission of the Office of Public Works

The Publishers have made every reasonable effort to contact the copyright holders of material reproduced in this book. If any infringement of copyright has occurred, the owners of such copyright are requested to contact the Publishers.

Contents

Chapter 1	The Church Yesterday and Today	5
Chapter 2	Giving a Soul to Modern Society	22
Chapter 3	The Church: The Parable of God	39
Chapter 4	Introduction to Morality	52
Chapter 5	What is Truth?	61
Chapter 6	The Call of Conscience	72
Chapter 7	The Sacrament of Reconciliation	82
Chapter 8	The Sacrament of Marriage	96

Prayer at Taizé

CHAPTER 1

The Church Yesterday and Today

> This chapter traces the history of the Church both in Europe and in Ireland. It observes the images of the Church through the ages. In particular, it analyses why many people today have difficulty with the Church.

Introduction

In considering the theologian's position in the world today, the sociologist Harvey Cox, author of *The Secular City*, recalls a story told by the Danish philosopher Søren Kierkegaard.

According to this story, a travelling circus in Denmark had caught fire. The manager of the circus feared that the fire would spread to a nearby village, so he sent the clown, who was already dressed and made-up for his performance, to the village to warn the people. The clown ran to the village and called on the inhabitants to come and help put out the fire but no one heeded him. Rather, they applauded, interpreting his shouts as a brilliant piece of advertising designed to attract as many people as possible to the performance.
The clown continued to plead with the people, urging them to take him seriously and to accept that there really was a fire and they they were in danger. But the more earnest he became the more the villagers thought how splendidly he had played his role – until finally, it was too late for help and the fire engulfed the village, burning it to the ground as it had done the circus.

This story was used by Cox to describe the theologian's position in the world today, but it might equally be used to illustrate a perception of the Church, particularly in what we refer to as the western world.

While it has to be acknowledged that for almost two thousand years Christianity, as represented by the Churches, has fired the imagination of Europeans whose great cultural and intellectual achievements were all for the glory of God, there is much evidence that the authority and influence of the Catholic Church and, indeed, of all Churches is now waning. Sometimes it can seem that the Church resembles the clown who cannot make people listen to his message.

> In his medieval, or at any rate old-fashioned, clown's costume he is simply not taken seriously. Whatever he says, he is ticketed and classified, so to speak, by his role. Whatever he does in his attempts to demonstrate the seriousness of the position, people always know in advance that he is in fact just a clown. They are already familiar with what he is talking about and know that he is just giving a performance which has little or nothing to do with reality.
> *Introduction to Christianity*, Joseph Ratzinger

Something of the same sentiment is captured in Pádraig Daly's poem:

> Like old countrywomen
> by fireplaces on winter evenings
> we sit alone.
>
> Outside day draws in; dogs
> bark to one another across acres
> of mountain; the last red hen
> goes wearily to shelter; younger
> voices rise and fall in laughter
> or argument; there is banging of churns
> and milk poured quietly.
>
> We have some urgent tale to tell
> about life; but our mouths open
> and no sound gathers shape.
> We belong out by the side of things.
> Sagart 3

While the Church has been no stranger to criticism and hostility, the growing sense of indifference towards the Church is a relatively new phenomenon. Equally,

> what is new and surprising is that the criticism today levelled at Roman Catholicism is widely voiced by Roman Catholics.
> *The Role of the Christian Today*, J.P. Kenny

Questions
1. Do you agree with Ratzinger's idea that for many people today the Church is out of touch with reality? Why do you think this is so?
2. What image of priesthood is captured in Pádraig Daly's poem?

Consider the following statements on the Church:

1. I believe in God – it's the Church I have problems with.
2. Everybody needs guidance; that's why the Church is there.
3. There is so much happening in the Church, you couldn't believe in it.
4. The Church is good in some respects when it reminds people of the poor and the Third World, but it shouldn't interfere in people's lives on things like divorce and contraception.
5. Nobody cares about the Church today. They are too busy getting on with their own lives. The Church is a thing of the past.
6. In this country, the Church is a very powerful institution and has a lot of control over schools and hospitals. The Church should concentrate on religious issues.
7. I think the Church is good. It reminds people that there is something more to life.
8. The Church has lasted so long, there must be something to it.
9. The Church makes no impact on my life. I find the Mass very boring.
10. The Church is very negative about women. How can it talk about not discriminating against blacks, for instance, when it does not allow women priests?
11. The Church is very wealthy. It should sell off its wealth and feed the poor.
12. The Church is made up of bishops and priests who are totally conservative and know nothing about people's lives.
13. You cannot be religious on your own. You need other people who believe. That is what the Church is for.
14. I would not like to see the Church fade away. It is very good for older people but young people find it boring.

Exercise

1. In the first column tick the statement(s) you identify with.

2. In the second column indicate the understanding of Church which each statement reflects, e.g. the Church as institution; the Church as community; the Church as teacher; the Church as the people of God; the Church as hierarchy; etc.

3. Which image of the Church do you believe in most strongly? Which image would you like to believe in? Which image do you think most people believe in?

Emperor Constantine

The way things were – A European perspective

Since the year 313AD, when the Roman Emperor Constantine put an end to the laws against Christians, Christianity in one form or another has not just influenced but dominated almost every aspect of human life in Europe. Constantine saw himself as the ruler of the Church as well as of the Empire and his successors made Christianity the official religion of the Roman Empire.

> During the **Dark Ages** and the barbarian invasions which brought an end to the Roman Empire there was only one institution which kept the light of civilisation flickering in the darkness. That was the Church.
> *The Christian Heritage*, Desmond Forristal

By the **Middle Ages**, the Church had come to dominate every aspect of European life – art, architecture, literature, music, education, and even leisure. Europe had become Christendom – the realm, the kingdom of Christians. The link between Church and crown was now firmly established.

The **Renaissance and Reformation** brought the Middle Ages to an end. Two seemingly contradictory features concerning the Church emerge at this time. On the one hand, the Renaissance figures who drew much of their inspiration from ancient Greece and Rome were often supported by popes and cardinals who seemed more interested in pagan art than in reform of the Church. On the other hand, the Renaissance produced some of the greatest religious art ever created.

The recognition that the Church badly needed to be reformed expressed itself in two contrasting ways.

1. The Protestant Reformation, as we know it, began on 31 October 1517, when Martin Luther nailed his document to the door of Wittenburg Cathedral. This was the beginning of a series of attacks on the Church which resulted in the division of the Church of Rome into the Catholic Church and the various Protestant Churches.

2. The Catholic or Counter-Reformation of the sixteenth century was the Catholic Church's attempt to reform itself. The Council of Trent, which lasted from December 1545 until 1563, concerned itself firstly with Catholic teaching – the restatement of the truths of Christian faith, many of which had been challenged by the Protestant reformers. Secondly, the Council of Trent was concerned with the reform of Church life. Education of the clergy and a renewal of the spiritual foundations of religious life received great emphasis. The bishops who returned from Trent to their own dioceses began the most significant reform the Church had seen in three hundred years.

The main feature of the eighteenth century was the **Enlightenment**, which not only challenged all sources of authority – the monarchy as well as the Church – but also questioned the very faith which the Church professed in the first place. The emphasis was on reason rather than faith as the guiding principle in everything.

The Enlightenment helped to bring about the French Revolution and the collapse of the monarchy. While the monarchy was restored after the fall of Napoleon in 1815, the nineteenth century saw a number of revolutions throughout Europe which gradually stripped the kings of their power and transferred it to the people. Christianity, however, seemed to be stronger than ever during the nineteenth century. The challenge to faith posed by the philosophers of the Enlightenment seemed to have been forgotten, at least temporarily:

Martin Luther preaching, engraving by Gustav König

Mock on, mock on, Voltaire, Rousseau:
Mock on, mock on: 'tis all in vain!
You throw the sand against the wind,
And the wind blows it back again.

And every sand becomes a gem
Reflected in the beams divine;
Blown back they blind the mocking eye,
But still in Israel's path they shine.

The atoms of Democritus
And Newton's particles of light
Are sands upon the Red Sea shore,
Where Israel's tents do shine so bright.
    William Blake, 1757–1827

The **nineteenth century** posed more problems for the Church than for Christianity:
> Churches failed to see that the passing of the old monarchies was a liberation for the Churches. They had become so accustomed to the close link between Church and the crown that they felt threatened by the coming of democracy.
> *The Christian Heritage*

The **twentieth century**, on the other hand, has witnessed an attack on the whole question of faith as well as on the authority of the Church. The ideas first put forward by the Enlightenment re-emerged and were strengthened by the scientific and industrial revolutions, the rise of socialism and the development of pluralist socialism – all of which in one way or another have called into question the role of religion and the Church in the modern world (see *Reason to Believe*, chapters 1 & 2). However, as we approach the end of the twentieth century, it seems that people have more difficulty with the Church than with belief in God as such.

Some recent evidence

In 1981 a group of academics surveyed the values and the attitudes of the members of the European Community. In 1990 they were joined by other academics to complete the largest survey ever carried out on what people think. It examined people's attitudes and values in relation to work, politics, trade unions and marriage, as well as religious and moral issues. In the summer of 1994, the Second European Values Survey was published.

Among many other things this survey reveals some paradoxical attitudes towards the Church and religion.

While there is a substantial rejection of conventional religion and its expression in religious practice, there is no corresponding decline in personal spirituality. At the same time, people by and large still insist on Church practice for rites of passage such as birth, marriage and death, but have more confidence in the European Community, in the social security system, in the education system and in major companies than in the Church.

In the ten years since the previous survey, public confidence in every institution has been falling. There has been a marked decline in confidence in democratic institutions like governments, trade unions, the press and the legal system, but the most marked decline of all has been in institutions of authority like the Church, the armed forces and the police. There is a general acceptance that the Church has a contribution to make to public debate but the extent of that contribution depends on the issue. For instance:

> 60% believe that the Church should speak out on Third World issues and racial discrimination.
> 50% believe that the Church should voice its opinion on disarmament, ecological issues, unemployment, euthanasia and abortion.
> 22% believe that the Church should have something to say about government policy.
> 66% believe it *inappropriate* for the Church to speak out on homosexuality or extra-marital affairs.

Interpreting the evidence

1. DISENCHANTMENT WITH INSTITUTIONS

One of the interesting facts to emerge from this survey, which seems to be substantiated by other sources which gauge people's attitudes towards religion and the Church, is that people have a bigger problem with the Church than with faith as such. In 1968 the theologian Joseph, later Cardinal, Ratzinger wrote:

> ...for many people today the Church has become the main obstacle to belief. They can no longer see in it anything but the human struggle for power, the petty spectacle of those who, with their claim to administer official Christianity, seem to stand most in the way of the true spirit of Christianity.
> *Introduction to Christianity*

However, the Church is not the only institution to evoke negative reaction today. There is a growing disenchantment with institutions in general.

> There is a cynicism abroad which suspects every structure, every group, every organisation. Whether it is politicians or clergy, public servants or journalists, employers or union officials, nobody is presumed to be acting with integrity or from unselfish motives.
> *Life in all its Fullness*, Donal Murray

It is easy to become cynical about institutions which are perceived to be corrupt. Looking specifically at the Church as institution, it is easy to cite examples from history which are so filled with human failure that some people wonder if the Church has not betrayed the cause of Christ.

> At various times, popes, bishops, clergy, religious and layfolk, have given scandalous example. From the long history of Roman Catholicism it is easy to pick out plenty of examples of discord between practice and preaching. Too often Roman Catholicism has figured as tyrant, Grand Inquisitor, shopkeeper, rather than servant... One recalls Pietro Ottoboni: on 6 October, 1689, at the age of nearly 80, he became Alexander VIII. During his brief pontificate of sixteen months he found little opportunity for doing good except to his own relatives. A contemporary remarked that with Alexander, the devil of nepotism was again on horseback at home. He gave a Cardinal's hat to his 22-year-old nephew and allowed him to collect a revenue amounting to 80,000 crowns.
> *The Role of the Christian Today*

The Church, along with other institutions, has been no stranger to scandals and abuses, but, as Bishop Donal Murray notes:

> ...that alone does not explain the transformation in attitudes which we have experienced in the last couple of decades. Something more fundamental is at stake. We are seeing a collapse of the sense of being part of a common effort and of pursuing a common goal.

Institutions and organisations, be they political parties, trade unions or the Church, depend on a shared vision or a common goal for their very existence. Indeed, they only come to be in the first place because people have a shared vision which draws them together. The motivating factor in being committed to an organisation or institution and in working on its behalf is the pursuit of a common goal. When people do not have such a shared vision or common goal they see institutions as impersonal and out of touch with their individual hopes and dreams, cares and concerns.

According to Bishop Murray, there is an absence of a shared vision in Ireland and indeed throughout Europe today. In this country, until recent times, there was
> …a consensus on what we stood for, on what being Irish meant, on the kind of values we wished to implement.

Nowadays, the problem is
> …not simply that our shared values as a nation have changed, it is that in many ways we are no longer operating out of any shared vision. One wonders if anything really unites us apart from cheering for Jack's Army!

2. THE RISE OF INDIVIDUALISM AND THE BREAKDOWN OF COMMUNITY

> There is no such thing as society – there are individual men and women and there are families.
> *Margaret Thatcher*

In an article on Thatcherism and Reaganism in *The Irish Times,* Paul Smyth wrote:
> The reason that increasing numbers of Americans do not vote is because they are alienated not from the political process or politicians, but from a whole range of socially co-operative behaviour; or, in effect, from the idea of participating in social activities or society itself. The willingness of the individual to see himself as part of the collective to whom he owes responsibility is gradually being whittled away.

What we sometimes describe in this country as the 'mé féin' mentality, or the emphasis on the individual and his or her concerns (the philosophy which lies behind what became known as Thatcherism and Reaganism), otherwise known as individualism, has its origins in mid-nineteenth-century Britain during the industrial revolution, which caused a massive movement of people from the country to the towns in search of work. Life in the country was locally and community orientated. People knew each other and knew about one another's cares and concerns. Life in a large town or city was a very different experience. Everything was bigger, more impersonal and anonymous. In such an environment it is difficult to foster a community spirit. It was no wonder that the Church, which had long been rooted in the country and in the community, would find difficulty in this changed situation.

Today, many people have become absorbed in their own private concerns – their health, their bodies, their homes, their families. Indeed the emphasis on the individual and on

his/her happiness is so great that in the words of one writer:
> ...every sharing of common purpose appears to be a diminishment of individuality.
> *Knowledge and Politics*, R. Unger

It is no wonder then that for many people, religion has become a private rather than a community matter. Moreover, our western emphasis on individual fulfilment sees religion as a source of inner comfort rather than of gospel challenge. Perhaps this is why it is easier to believe in a God who is seen as the fulfilment of our longings rather than in a Church that is seen to be making demands on our lives. Perhaps, too, this is one of the reasons why the Church seems more relevant in the developing world, where people have managed to keep alive that sense of community and shared vision that is often lost in our First World.

3. THE 'NEW TYPE OF CATHOLIC'

The European Values Survey (1994) reveals that the majority of people surveyed believe that the Church should speak out on matters like the Third World and racial discrimination, but think it inappropriate for it to speak on matters that pertain to their private lives, e.g. homosexuality and extra-marital affairs.

This finding is in line with the findings of the previous survey which showed that people have the highest levels of belief in teachings like the Assumption of Our Lady (92%) and the Trinity (94%), but have grave difficulties with some of the moral teachings of the Church on matters like divorce and contraception, which affect their personal and private lives.

Moreover, over one third reported that religious principles seldom, if ever, guide their behaviour. Such findings, according to Professor Liam Ryan, point to the emergence of
> ...a new type of Catholic, as yet in the minority... characterised by an informed appreciation of the value of the supernatural and sacramental life of the Church, but retaining an independence of mind – largely on moral matters. The new Catholic demands that the Church speak more authoritatively and more often on matters of social morality but, at the same time, questions the Church's authority to speak on moral matters which affect his/her private life. Such Catholics are often liberal on sexual and marital questions but, at the same time, can be quite adamant about rejecting abortion... (they) continue to seek sacramental ministry from the Church at times when such ministry seems appropriate or necessary.... All want a more pastoral and less authoritarian style of Church leadership. Above all, they like the newer theology which suggests that it is hard, rather than easy, for a reasonably religious person to commit a mortal sin.
> 'Faith under Survey', *The Furrow*

This 'new type of Catholic' calls to mind Fluther in *The Plough and the Stars*:
> I think we ought to have as great a regard for religion as we can, so as to keep it out of as many things as possible!

Exercise

1. What institutions do you support? Why?

2. Is it true to say that there is a much greater emphasis on the individual than on the community today?

3. Could you be described as one of the new types of Catholic? Why?

The Church in Ireland – a unique experience

St Molaise

Chapter 1 of *Reason to Believe* identified some of the features which characterised the early Irish experience of Christianity: the natural religious sense found in the Celtic people even before Christianity; the experience of God as being close to one's life; the awareness of God's presence in nature; the link between love of God and love of one's neighbour; a keen interest in Scripture; the importance of pilgrimage; the attraction of monastic life with its emphasis on learning, on prayer, on fasting and on penance – those more ascetic and mysterious aspects of human experience.

THE 'CELTIC' CHURCH

In a study of Irish Catholicism, the Redemptorist priest John J. Ó Ríordáin traces the story of Christianity and the Church from its Celtic origins to the present day.

> The Church as established by St Patrick and other missionaries was very similar to that which was found in the rest of Europe at the time. However, by the middle of the sixth century, this largely diocesan structure was replaced by a monastic system which became so widespread that …ultimately Ireland became unique in Western Christendom in having most of its more important Churches ruled by a monastic hierarchy, many of whom were not bishops.
>
> *Irish Catholics,* John J. Ó Ríordáin

The emphasis on the monastic community rather than on the diocese resulted in an experience of Church that was very much locally based. This in turn fostered that other unique feature of Christianity as it developed in Ireland, namely 'muintearas', or community-mindedness. The late

Cardinal Tomás Ó Fiaich noted that:
> A sixth century monastery must not be pictured as one of the great medieval monasteries on the continent. It was much closer in appearance to the monastic settlements of the Nile valley or the island of Lerins than to later Monte Cassino or Clairvaux. Even the Latin word monasterium, when borrowed into Irish under the form 'muintir', was applied not to the buildings but to the community.
>   'The Beginnings of Christianity' in *The Course of Irish History*,
>   ed. T.W. Moody and F.X. Martin

Such an experience of Church was personal and intimate, fostering a sense of belonging and of participation. Perhaps the weakness of this early Church was that it lacked the structure and organisation which might have ensured its greater permanence.

THE MEDIEVAL PERIOD

The monastic system was largely brought to an end by the Viking raids. In the early twelfth century a national synod held near Cashel, Co. Tipperary, divided Ireland into dioceses, similar to those found in Europe, which have more or less continued to the present day.

Despite some abuses which led to the need for reform during this period, and despite the unrest caused by the Norman invasion, the older hallmarks of early Christianity – asceticism, hospitality, devotion to Mary, pilgrimage, prayer and fasting – survived. Thus there was a natural link between religion and life in all its aspects.

A typical penal law (1739)

THE REFORMATION

When the Reformation began in Europe in the sixteenth century, it left Ireland largely unaffected. There was little if any awareness in Ireland of the abuses that led to this upheaval of the Church on the continent. Indeed, as Fr Canice Mooney notes:
> Far from feeling any resentment about papal aggression, the average native Irishman of standing or education welcomed the fact that over and above the King of England stood the common father of Christendom, to whom in the last resort all could appeal for justice.
> *Irish Ecclesiastical Record*, Vol. 99, 1963

The Reformation in England, however, was to have a profound effect on Ireland. The desire to change Ireland's religion as well as her language, culture and tradition, was part of the process of anglicisation, the ultimate aim of which was the conquest of Ireland. The various attempts to change the Irish religion, which culminated in the Penal Laws, resulted in the close identification between Irish nationalism and Irish Catholicism. As Europe was beginning to experience a certain separation between Church and State, Ireland began to see what was almost a fusion between religion and nationality. The terms could almost be interchanged: Irish and Catholic; English and Protestant.

A persecuted Church is almost always a more fervent one. The Penal Laws against Catholicism in Ireland strengthened the people's devotion.

> Fidelity to the Mass was the aspect of the faith which outshone all other expressions of it in the penal times. The seventeenth and eighteenth centuries were noted as the age of the Mass-rock. It was the age of the 'Sagart aroon' (the darling priest), as the people affectionately designated their pastor. They sheltered him at the risk of life and limb; by night he ministered to them and, in the remote caves and bogs, in a shack or beside a fence on a boulder or rock, he would celebrate the outlawed Mass.
> *Irish Catholics*

THE NINETEENTH CENTURY

The most profound change in sixteen hundred years in the Church and Christianity in Ireland took place during the nineteenth century. The anglicisation of Ireland, while it did not deter the Catholic faith, did succeed in replacing the Irish language with English and in introducing a somewhat puritanical Anglo-Saxon culture, with its emphasis on middle-class morality. Much of this foreign culture was embraced enthusiastically by a rising Catholic middle-class in Ireland who identified things English with progress and prosperity.

The net effect of this new culture was that it left the majority of the people without a culturally familiar natural mode of expression. This, together with the importation of various forms of prayer and religious practice from the continent (novenas, stations of the cross, missions, etc.), led to a more formal and sometimes more impersonal style of religious practice that was new and foreign to the Irish psyche.

> One is loth to be critical of so venerable a corpus of prayer and piety, but one may most respectfully suggest that it may be too sustained where it should be a little more spontaneous, too civilised and urban where it should be a bit bedraggled and daring and rural, too elaborate where it should be inspired, too flat and level where it should be soaring to the skies, too articulate and too fully stated for the Celtic mentality for which, as Kuno Meyer said, the 'half-said thing is dearest'.
> 'Patterns of Prayer and Devotion 1750–1850', T. de Bhál, in *Studies in Pastoral Liturgy*, ed. Dom Placid Murray OSB

W.B. Yeats was of a similar mind when he wrote 'The Fiddler of Dooney':

> When I play on my fiddle in Dooney,
> Folk dance like the wave of the sea;
> My cousin is priest in Kilvarnet;
> My brother in Mocharabuiee.
>
> I passed my brother and cousin:
> They read in their books of prayer;
> I read in my book of songs
> I bought at the Sligo fair.
>
> When we come to the end of time
> To Peter sitting in state,
> He will smile at the three old spirits,
> But call me first through the gate.
>
> For the good are always the merry,
> Save by an evil chance,
> And the merry love the fiddle,
> And the merry love the dance:
>
> And when the folk there spy me,
> They will all come up to me,
> With 'Here is the fiddler of Dooney',
> And dance like the wave of the sea.

STRUCTURAL REFORM

The other major legacy of the nineteenth century has to do with the organisational and institutional aspects of the Church. At this time the faith of the people was strong. They had proven this during the Penal Days. But the Church, having been persecuted for so long, was in need of much structural reform.

After the granting of Catholic Emancipation in 1829, the Church was free to set about this task, which was largely initiated and carried through by Cardinal Cullen. He was determined to build an organised and disciplined Church and he succeeded largely in doing this. There was much reform of the clergy and there was a major emphasis on the sacraments, especially Mass attendance, which increased from between 30 per cent and 40 per cent to over 90 per cent in fifty years. The net result of this emphasis was that

> …the great mass of the Irish people became practising Catholics, which they have uniquely and essentially remained both at home and abroad down to the present day.
>
> *American Historical Review,* Vol 77, 1972

Pilgrims praying at the grotto in Lourdes

THE TWENTIETH CENTURY

This brief glance at the history of the Irish Church provides an insight into the kind of Church we have inherited in the twentieth century. Two images emerge.

1. A Church based on a natural lively sense of faith and which was community orientated.

2. More recently, a Church which became somewhat more institutionalised and formal and linked with the idea of Irish nationalism. This Church was to last until the 1960s when nationalism became less important and Ireland was exposed to those influences which have challenged faith and the Church in other countries.

As we approach the end of the twentieth century, different perspectives of the Church in Ireland emerge:

1. There is an extraordinarily high level of Church attendance, yet closer analysis often reveals a certain lack of understanding or of conviction. For young people, especially, Mass attendance is often the result of mere habit or conformity to the expectation of parents, parish or school. There has been a marked decline in participation in the Sacrament of Reconciliation, which might demand a more personal commitment.

2. In the minds of many, the Church is identified with moral pronouncements which are often seen as negative and as intrusive in the areas of personal freedom and the quest for happiness.

3. The Church as institution evokes some mixed reactions. (a) There are those, particularly the unemployed, who see the Church as being on the side of the middle classes. They often perceive it as ranking alongside other institutions like the health boards, the Department of Social Welfare and the government, and thus see it as a bureaucratic organisation and feel alienated from it. (b) There are those who resent what they perceive to be the all-too-pervasive power and influence of the Church in matters like education and health care, which they claim should be the concern of the State only. (c) At the other end of the scale, there are those who feel that the Church has 'gone soft' since Vatican II. They would like to see her speak out more often, especially on sin. Some would like to see Church law enshrined in State law and a return to a closer link between Church and State.

4. There is another group which senses something of what the Church is about and tries to recapture some of those earlier experiences which made the link between faith and Church more personal and more meaningful – the attraction of small-group Masses (e.g. Taizé) and prayer and Bible groups, and the numbers of pilgrims to places like Lough Derg all bear witness to this.

SUMMARY CHART	The Church in Europe
a. Constantine – The Dark Ages	a. Church as the symbol of civilisation
b. The Middle Ages	b. Europe as Christendom
c. The Renaissance & Reformation	c. Religious art Protestant Churches Counter-Reformation
d. The Enlightenment	d. Challenge to faith and to Church authority
e. The Nineteenth Century	e. Problems for the Church rather than for faith
f. The Twentieth Century European Values Survey	f. Attacks on faith and on the authority of the Church Disenchantment with institutions Rise of individualism and the breakdown of community The 'new type of Catholic'

SUMMARY CHART	The Church in Ireland
a. The Celtic Church	a. Emphasis on monasticism Sense of community Church as local and personal
b. The Medieval Period	b. Ireland was divided into dioceses Religion and life still linked
c. The Reformation	c. Little awareness of Church abuses in Ireland Penal Laws, emphasis on the Mass Link between Catholicism and Nationalism
d. The Nineteenth Century	d. Major changes in the Church in Ireland More formal style of religious practice Puritan morality Church became organised and institutionalised
e. The Twentieth Century	e. High level of Church practice still Negative attitudes towards the Church as teacher Commitment to life in the Church

Revision questions and exercises

1. What does this brief study of the Church in Europe tell you about the role of the Church?
2. Why, in your opinion, has the Church become irrelevant for many people?
3. What do you find attractive about the early Irish Church? Is there any sense of this early Church still to be found today?

CHAPTER 2

Giving a Soul to Modern Society

> Chapter 2 examines why faith needs to be embodied in a Church. It examines the role of the Church as the call to give a soul to modern society. It considers some models of the Church and the question of the sinful Church.

Introduction: The disturbing Gospel

That the Church should come in for criticism today should, in one way, come as no surprise to us. However justified criticism of the Church may be with regard to its sinfulness, it is equally true that those who challenge the prevailing attitudes and actions of people and call for a change of heart have always been perceived as 'voices crying in the wilderness'. The prophets of the Old Testament who, in times of plenty, called on the people to abandon their idolatrous ways were frequently rejected. The prophet Hosea rebuked the people:

> Sons of Israel, listen to the word of Yahweh, for Yahweh indicts the inhabitants of the country: there is no fidelity, no tenderness, no knowledge of God in the country, only perjury and lies, slaughter, theft, adultery and violence, murder after murder. That is why the country is in mourning, and all who live in it pine away. *4:1-3*

But the people did not want to listen:
> The prophet is mad, Israel protests, this inspired fellow is raving. *9:7*

The prophet Micah met with a similar reaction.

> Do not rave, they rave,
> do not rave like this.
> No shame is going to overtake us.
> Can the House of Jacob be accursed?
> Has Yahweh lost patience?
> Is that his way of going to work?
> Surely his words are words of kindness for his people Israel? *2:6-7*

The cosy kind of religion that appealed to the people of Israel is often the kind of religion to which people are attracted today. Religion can meet many needs of people – the need to find meaning of some sort, the need for social acceptability, the need to be able to identify with something, to feel part of a group or organisation, to find a certain kind of security. This is the kind of religion which

> acknowledges God but does not, in practice, see any connection between the Creator and most of life's events and decisions
> *Can These Bones Live?* Donal Murray

Jesus Christ was very disturbing. He challenged not just the way people looked at reality, but also the way they lived their lives. We remember the story of the rich young man in Matthew's Gospel:

> Once a man came to Jesus. 'Teacher', he asked, 'what good things must I do to receive eternal life?' 'Why do you ask me concerning what is good?' answered Jesus. 'There is One who is good. Keep the commandments if you want to enter life.' 'What commandments?' he asked. Jesus answered, 'Do not murder; do not commit adultery; do not accuse anyone falsely; respect your father and mother; and love your neighbour as you love yourself.' 'I have obeyed all these commandments,' the young man replied. 'What else do I need to do?' Jesus said to him, 'If you want to be perfect, go and sell all you have and give your money to the poor, and you will have riches in heaven; then come and follow me.' When the young man heard this, he went away sad, because he was very rich. Jesus then said to his disciples, 'I assure you: it will be very hard for rich people to enter the Kingdom of heaven. I repeat: it is much harder for a rich man to enter the Kingdom of God than for a camel to go through the eye of a needle.' *19:16-24*

Question
Do you find the Gospel call disturbing? Explain.

The Church is called to give a soul to modern society

Some people have difficulty with the Church because of their failure to recognise the vision out of which she is operating. Too often, all that is heard is the Church's negative stance on a particular issue or action, without an understanding of the rationale that lies behind it. Indeed much of what the Church stands for makes little sense to those operating out of a different vision of human life and destiny. After all, many of the Gospel values proclaimed by Jesus Christ turn the values of the world upside down.

> He who exalts himself shall be humbled.
> He who loses his life shall find it.

The Church exists to prompt people, to call us to a way of life that is inspired by the vision of humanity as, ultimately, God-orientated.

> The less we understand ourselves and our human dignity, the less we understand the Church. *Can These Bones Live?*

Without some appreciation and belief in the dignity and nature of humanity within the Christian vision it is difficult to understand what the Church is about.

Chapter 4 of *Reason to Believe* examined the 'modern search for a soul' which recognises that people today have become somewhat disenchanted with the promises of this century, and are searching for something else. The glorious future anticipated by science and technology, capitalism, secularism and humanism, has failed to materialise for many people. It was suggested that this is because

> it is not possible to understand man on the basis of economics alone, nor to define him simply on the basis of class membership. *Centesimus annus*, 24

Many of the 'isms', the ideologies of this century, promised happiness without reference to the divine, but as Pope John Paul II, commenting on the demise of communism, writes:

> Marxism had promised to uproot the need for God from the human heart, but the results have shown that it is not possible to succeed in this without throwing the human heart into turmoil. *CA*, 24

The essence of the Church's teaching, indeed the reason for its very existence and the vision which inspires it, is the belief that human beings are more than economic, political or even social entities – that the truth about humanity is its transcendent or divine nature – its soul.

> In your nature, O eternal God-head, I know my own nature. *St Catherine of Siena*

Very often, however, modern society loses sight of its ultimate nature and purpose and

settles for something less. In the words of D. H. Lawrence:
> Man has little needs and deeper needs. We have fallen into the mistake of living from our little needs till we have almost lost our deeper needs in a sort of madness.

Christianity's basic message, and it is the Church's task to proclaim it, is that the ultimate destiny of humankind is with God. That is why 'a human being cannot give himself to a purely human plan for reality'. (*CS* 41) Even if a magic wand were waved in the morning, and problems like unemployment, oppression and violence were solved, it still would not result in ultimate human happiness, even though it may appear so at first glance. This is because there is a part of human nature – what we call the soul – which seeks a deeper and more ultimate fulfilment.

At the same time, Christianity is no flight from the world. Rather, its message is the Gospel:
> …The good news that the world as we know it – with all its sufferings and injustices and deprivations for so many people – is not the world as God intends it and promises it to us.
> *What Are The Theologians Saying Now?* Monica Hellwig

The Christian is called to be part of the counter-movement against the sufferings and problems of the world. This requires a fundamental change of heart on our part.

> If the present systems generated by the human 'heart' turn out to be incapable of ensuring peace, then it is the human 'heart' that must be renewed, in order to renew systems, institutions and methods. Christian faith has a word for this fundamental change of heart: it is called 'conversion'.
> *Message for the World Day of Peace, Pope John Paul II*, 1983, par. 3

The challenge to bring about change in the world may generate a certain feeling of helplessness in us, yet,

> The one area where nobody is helpless is in changing their own attitudes. Without that change, any attempt to come to grips with the problems of society and the world is hypocritical, shallow and doomed. That conversion is the vital, and powerful, first step. There is no other path to the humanisation of society and the world except the one that begins with an individual change of heart.
> *The Church – Guardian of Freedom,* Donal Murray

Such a change of heart calls into question those things which the world values. Thus:
> Money and power and prestige will find no place in God's Kingdom except to the extent that they have been used to express and build love between people and with God.
> *The Church – Guardian of Freedom*

The Church: the embodiment of faith

There are many who are attracted by the faith vision that is the foundation of the Church but who question the need for a Church as such. Sometimes they accept the 'cause' of Jesus but object to what believers have made of this 'cause'. The organisation and structures of the Church seem to them to be more of an impediment than an aid to faith. Sometimes they question why faith needs a Church. Is it not possible to relate to God and to try to live as good a life as possible?

Such a position often seems noble and attractive yet closer examination reveals elements of the individualism referred to in chapter 1. Sometimes people prefer a 'private Christianity' because they don't want demands to be made on them. They do not want to move outside their own concerns to the wider concerns of the community. 'Me and God' can be very cosy and very undemanding. Yet the idea of Christianity on one's own is a contradiction in terms. The essence of Christianity is love, and love by definition is relational. It goes outside of self to another. Christianity is not possible without reference to other people. Thus Christianity demands a community experience of some sort. The Church – the Christian community – came to be in the first place because of those who shared the vision of life as presented by Jesus. The hallmark of this early community, that which differentiated them from other peoples, was the care and concern they had for each other.

> See those Christians, see how they love one another.

In his book, *Introduction to Christian Faith*, the theologian Walter Kasper puts forward the following reasons for having a Church:
> Christianity without a Church is a utopian fantasy. Christian religious conviction, like other human beliefs, could not survive for long without some degree of institutionalisation.

In other words, the institution makes such beliefs concrete and lasting. It spells out what those beliefs are and describes the kind of behaviour that should result from them. Christianity without a Church would be like the human spirit without the human body. The traditions, the teachings and the actions of the Church are, so to speak, the flesh and blood of Christianity. They are the visible, tangible form of the Christian vision.

1. Without the challenge of the Churches, which constantly keep alive the memory of the source of Jesus Christ, Christianity wouldn't be likely to survive for more than one or two generations at the most – that is to say, the Church is the living witness of a kingdom of God as proclaimed by Jesus. In this sense, then, the Church is the historical continuation of Christ in and through the community of those who believe in him.

2. How could Christianity carry on in a world of powerful and overpowering institutions if it did not become institutionalised? In other words, how could Christianity challenge the vision and the value systems of world institutions like governments if it were just an abstract ideal? Indeed, it may well be true to say that the more powerful the Church as institution is the more likely it will be listened to by other powerful and influential institutions.

3. How would the individual Christian carry on believing – we have to put it as strongly as that – if he wasn't carried by the strength of people's faith? Indeed, a person comes to Christian faith in the first place because he/she sees it believed, lived, proclaimed and practised in the Churches.
Introduction to Christian Faith

The Church: the embodiment of faith

1. INTRODUCTION: THE CHURCH'S UNDERSTANDING OF ITSELF

The word 'Church' (Latin *ecclesia* from the Greek *ek-kalein*, 'to call out of') means a convocation or an assembly. It designates the assemblies of the people, usually for a religious purpose. *Ekklesia* is used frequently in the Greek Old Testament for the assembly of the Chosen People before God…. By calling itself 'Church', the first community of Christian believers recognised itself as heir to that assembly.
Catechism of the Catholic Church, 751

Ecclesiology is the branch of theology which studies the Church. It is interesting to note that ecclesiology is a somewhat recent development in that the Church did not begin to reflect upon itself until the late Middle Ages and only then because of certain conflicts which included the split between the Eastern and Western Churches.

The reason for the late development of ecclesiology was that the Church always saw the 'cause' of Jesus, rather than itself, as its primary concern. The salvation promised by Jesus, the establishment of the Kingdom of God on earth, and the call to conversion were what the Church was all about. The early Church's understanding of itself is expressed in the

Apostles' Creed, which distinguishes between faith in God, in Christ and in the Spirit and only then in the Church. Thus the Church is not the object of faith in the same way that God, Jesus Christ and the Spirit are. It is the continuation of the saving action of Jesus in history. In that sense it is an event

> ...in which the truth, freedom and justice which entered the world with Christ remain alive in history and are constantly given new life.
> *Introduction to Christian Faith*

The way in which the early Church speaks of itself illustrates this point: the most frequently used phrases are 'Church of God'; 'People of God'; 'Body of Christ'.

At the same time, just as we cannot separate the person of Jesus from the 'cause' of Jesus, so too we cannot separate the 'cause' of the Church from its physical form – the institution of the Church in the world. Thus the Church is not just the bearer of the good news of salvation, it is also the place where salvation is taking place right here and now. St Luke's description of the early Church in the Acts of the Apostles illustrates something of 'faith in action'.

> Many of them believed his message and were baptised, and about three thousand people were added to the group that day. They spent their time in learning from the apostles, taking part in the fellowship and sharing in the fellowship meals and the prayers. Many

miracles and wonders were being done through the apostles, and everyone was filled with awe. All the believers continued together in close fellowship and shared their belongings with one another. They would sell their property and possessions and distribute the money among them, according to what each one needed. Day after day they met as a group in the Temple, and they had their meals together in their homes, eating with glad and humble hearts, praising God and enjoying the good will of all the people. And every day the Lord added to their group those who were being saved. *2:41-47*

It is clear from this description of the early Church that the Church does not exist simply to call people to a way of life that is inspired by Christ. Through gathering for prayer, through sharing possessions, through being fired by a common vision, *the Church is the kingdom of God on earth being realised here and now.*

2. THE FOUNDING OF THE CHURCH

The death of Jesus left his followers dispirited, disorganised and somewhat lost. Many of them had been with him throughout his public ministry. They had been captivated by his words and deeds and promise of a glorious future. Now he was dead and the promise seemed hollow and empty. Had they, as often happens in life, been built up for something which was ultimately a pipe-dream?

If Christ has not been raised from the dead, your faith is in vain. *1 Co 15:16*

Not until Jesus had risen from the dead did the first Christians speak of a 'Church'. Three days after his death, the gospels tell us, Jesus rose from the dead and appeared to many of his followers – to Mary Magdalene and the group of women, to the apostles, and to the two disciples on the road to Emmaus. As soon as the disciples gathered

together with faith in the resurrection of the crucified Christ, the Church came into existence. The appearances of the Risen Christ together with the Pentecost experience convinced the disciples that while Jesus' earthly life and ministry were over, his work of salvation would continue through his followers. Thus Peter, speaking to the crowd following the Pentecost experience, could say:

'Listen to these words, fellow-Israelites! Jesus of Nazareth was a man whose divine authority was clearly proven to you by all the miracles and wonders which God performed through him… you killed him by letting sinful men crucify him. God has raised this very Jesus from death and we are all witnesses to this fact. He has been raised to the right hand side of God, his Father, and has received from him the Holy Spirit, as he had promised. What you see and hear is his gift that he has poured out on us…. All the people of Israel, then, are to know for sure that this Jesus, whom you crucified, is the one that God had made Lord and Messiah!' When the people heard this they were deeply troubled and said to Peter and the other apostles, 'What shall we do, brothers?' Peter said to them, 'Each one of you must turn away from his sins and be baptised in the name of Jesus Christ, so that your sins will be forgiven; and you will receive God's gift, the Holy Spirit.' *Acts 2:22-38*

With the Pentecost experience the work of the Church had begun. Moreover, what happened to a chosen few in a small room on that feast of Pentecost has been repeated over and over again throughout the history of the Church, albeit with less dramatic displays:

From the time of Jesus' death and Resurrection until today, people have been touched by his Spirit, and so they have gathered in communities of faith. In and through these communities, believers constantly grow in their understanding of Jesus' message. They also support one another as they try to live out the demands of their faith in their daily lives. These believers pray together, share their concerns and their gifts, and constantly call to mind and celebrate the powerful presence of the Lord in their midst. In doing so, the Church stands as a herald of the coming Kingdom of God, a messenger to the larger world of the coming reign of God that was announced by Jesus.
Understanding Catholic Christianity, Thomas Zanzig

3. MODELS OF THE CHURCH

In his opening address to the second session of Vatican II, Pope Paul VI declared:
The Church is a mystery. It is a reality imbued with the hidden presence of God. It lies, therefore, within the very nature of the Church to be always open to new and even greater exploration.
Council Speeches of Vatican II, ed. H. Kung, Y. Congar, D. O'Hanlon

Our western understanding of mystery as something unintelligible is not what is meant here. Rather, the term 'mystery', as applied to the Church, suggests that
…the Church is not fully intelligible to the finite mind of man, and that the reason for this lack of intelligibility is not the poverty but the richness of the Church itself.
Models of the Church, A. Dulles

In other words, as with the mystery of the human person, there are layers of meaning in the Church. Just as we never arrive at a position where we can say that we fully know another person, so too our knowledge of the Church will always be incomplete. Moreover, the fact that it is the Church of Christ adds to its mysterious nature. Thus, it is more helpful to talk about images or what one theologian calls 'models' of the Church. The Second Vatican Council used scriptural images to describe the Church:

…the inner nature of the Church is now made known to us in various images. Taken either from the life of the shepherd, or from cultivation of the land, from the art of building or from family life and marriage, these images have their preparation in the books of the prophets.
Lumen gentium, 6

The Vatican Council goes on to describe the Church as a sheepfold, a vineyard, as the building of God, as a mother and as a bride. The Church was also described as the People of God, the Body of Christ and as a sacrament. In *Models of the Church*, Avery Dulles selects five images to describe the nature of the Church and its mission.

1. *The Church as community (mystical communion)*

We have already said that the word 'Church' – *Ecclesia* – literally means assembly. This was the Christian community's first understanding of itself – a people called together because of their belief in God. What kind of community is the Church?

Sociologists today draw a distinction between two ways of being together in groups. Firstly, there is the formally organised or structured society like the State. It has its institutions and structures and is usually presided over by some ruling body like a government. Secondly, there is the more informal and personal grouping of people which we call community. It is characterised by a common vision which brings its members together in the first place.

Within such a community there is a concern not just for our own well-being but for that of the other members of the community also. There is a sharing of time and resources. While the law governs behaviour in the State by prohibiting the taking of another's life or property, for example, the community is much more concerned about what people can do for one another in a positive way. It is in this sense that the Church is described as a community – the People of God drawn together by belief in the resurrected Jesus.

The Church is not just a community in terms of the relationship between its members, it is also a community, a communion, in terms of its union with Christ. St Paul describes it as the Body of Christ:

> Christ is like a single body, which has many parts; it is still one body, even though it is made up of different parts. If one part of the body suffers, all the other parts suffer with it; if one part is praised, all the other parts share in its happiness. All of you are Christ's body, and each one is a part of it. *1 Co 12: 12. 26-27*

Thus there is the divine and the human element in the community we call the Church – the visible element of the people and the invisible Christ working through his body to continue the work of salvation.

2. *The Church as herald*

The people of the Middle Ages were more familiar with the person of the herald than we are today. At that time, when a king wanted to send an important message to his people, he sent a herald. The herald would ring a bell, blow a horn or shout to call the people together. Very often the herald wore special clothes so that the people recognised him as the king's representative who had been sent to them with a message. When the crowd had gathered and the people were quiet, the herald delivered his message.

In a similar way the Church has been described as the Herald of Christ. It is the official messenger, whose task it is to proclaim the word of God to all people in all places.
> …for we cannot but speak of what we have seen and heard. *Ac 4:20*

The Church has been commissioned by Jesus to be his herald:
> He said to them, 'Go into all the world and preach the gospel to the whole creation.'
> *Mk 16:15*

3. *The Church as sacrament*
> The Church's first purpose is to be the sacrament of the inner union of men with God. Because men's communion with one another is rooted in that union with God, the Church is also the sacrament of the unity of the human race.
> *Catechism of the Catholic Church, 775*

A sacrament is a special kind of sign. It does not just point towards something; it brings about or causes what it signifies. Just as a nation's flag is not just a symbol of a particular nation but also evokes a sense of belonging, of pride and of loyalty, so too a sacrament is not just a sign of God's presence, but makes God present here and now.

Jesus Christ was the sacrament of God. While here on earth he was the physical sign of God acting in the world. In the same way the Church is the sacrament of Christ which continues to be a sign of God's presence in the world. Through its sacraments, prayer, worship, good works and teachings the Church makes present God's saving action in the world.

4. *The Church as servant*

In Matthew's Gospel we read Jesus' perception of himself as one who
> …came not to be served but to serve, and to give his life as a ransom for many. *Mt 20:28*

Jesus came not just to proclaim the Kingdom of God but also to bring it about.
> He came to serve, to heal, to reconcile, to bind up wounds. Jesus, we may say, is in an exceptional way the Good Samaritan.
> *The Servant Church*, R. Cardinal Cushing

It is for this reason that
> …the Church announces the coming of the Kingdom not only in word through preaching and proclamation, but more particularly in work, in her ministry of reconciliation, of binding up wounds, of suffering service, of healing…. As the Lord was the 'man for others', so must the Church be 'the community for others'.
> *The Servant Church*

5.   *The Church as institution*

From the beginning, Christianity has always had an institutional side. As we have already observed, the Church of Christ could hardly carry out its mission without some stable organisational features.

> It could not unite men of many nations into a well-knit community of conviction, commitment, and hope, and could not minister effectively to the needs of mankind, unless it had responsible officers and properly approved procedures.
> *Models of the Church*

However, the institutional element of the Church is not to be confused with *institutionalis,* which sees institutionalism as the primary element in the Church, with its emphasis on power, influence and organisation. To do so would be to present,
> …the dry bones…without the sinews, flesh and spirit by which these bones live.
> *Can These Bones Live?*

Each of these five models or images of the Church captures something of what the Church is about. However, because the Church is a mystery, they do not fully represent all of what the Church is or is called to be. Moreover, any one model, taken on its own, without reference to the other images, results in a distortion of what the Church is. This frequently happens with the institutional model when people see the Church as institution only.
> They have not seen the other, deeper dimension of the Church's life, the living flesh on the structural bones. The structures exist in order to make that rich and varied life possible.
> *Can These Bones Live?*

Thus, any model of the Church is valid in so far as it witnesses to its purpose as initiated by Christ – namely the establishment of the Kingdom of God on earth. The Church's task is to proclaim this Kingdom and bring it about through its words and actions.

 **Exercise**
In groups, consider each of the five models of Church. Give examples of situations where the Church is acting out of each of these models.

The 'sinful' Church

The Creed describes the Church as holy: 'I believe in one holy, Catholic and apostolic Church.'

Yet, despite this, and despite all that has been said already about what the Church is and ought to be, there are many who see the Church as sinful rather than holy. This perception is enough to alienate them from what, in any event, they see as a distortion of what Jesus intended.

There is no defending much of the scandal that has been part and parcel of the history of the Church. It is very difficult for the Church itself when the ideal it professes is not matched by a corresponding way of life. The Irish Bishops drew attention to this in their Lenten Pastoral of 1980:

> The biggest obstacle to Christian faith today is not intellectual doubt. It is, quite simply, the unChristian life-style of many of us who think we are good Christians.
> *Handing on the Faith in the Home*

At the same time, we have to ask ourselves why people who have difficulty in living up to the Christian ideal themselves, still demand a perfect Church. Perhaps, once again, we have to go back to our very nature to discover an answer to this question. Pyschologists tell us that there is often a conflict in us between our ideal selves and our actual selves. We desire the ideal, but that often proves too difficult, so we tend to reduce the 'ideal' to the level at which we are comfortable. We live with this and yet there is a part of us that still longs for a higher, more perfect ideal, so we look for it outside ourselves. We look for the perfect friend, the perfect lover, the perfect child. It is quite natural that we should look for it in the Church too, because the Church professes an ideal for human destiny. With such a focus on the ideal there can often be the

> …bitterness of a heart which may perhaps have been disappointed in its high hopes and now, in the pain of wronged love, can see only the destruction of its hopes.
> *Introduction to Christianity*

While we may be lenient with ourselves we are often angry when our hopes are frustrated by people or things in which we have invested. This is often the syndrome which occurs at the end of the 'honeymoon period' in a marriage. We see the humanity and the imperfection of the other person. It is then that we choose either to abandon our spouse for failure to live up to our expectations, or else to accept and recognise his or her limitations as well as our own, and work together towards the betterment of each other.

The Church is not called holy because its members, individually and collectively, are holy, sinless people.

> …this dream, which appears afresh in every century, has no place in the waking world of our text, however movingly it may express a human longing which man will never abandon until a new heaven and a new earth really grant him what this age will never give him. Even at this point we can say that the sharpest critics of the Church in our time secretly live on this dream and, when they find it disappointed, bang the door of the house shut and denounce it as a deceit.
> *Introduction to Christianity*

The Church is holy because it is the Church of God, not because its members are perfect. It is holy because of the fidelity of God's invitation to us despite our sinfulness. Just as Jesus sat at the table with sinners and mingled with the misery of sin in the world, the Church too plunges itself into a sinful world, while at the same time calling that world out of its state of sinfulness. Thus there will always be the tension between the 'holy' and the 'unholy' Church – the ideal as presented by Christ and the frequent falling of his followers as they strive towards that ideal. This story illustrates how the Church – each one of us – is called to conversion over and over again.

> The story concerns a monastery that had fallen upon hard times. Once a great order, as a result of waves of anti-monastic persecution in the seventeenth and eighteenth centuries and the rise of secularism in the nineteenth, all its branch houses were lost and it had become decimated to the extent that there were only five monks left in the decaying mother house: the abbot and four others, all over seventy in age. Clearly it was a dying order.

In the deep woods surrounding the monastery there was a little hut that a rabbi from a nearby town occasionally used for a hermitage. Through their many years of prayer and contemplation the old monks had become a bit psychic, so they could always sense when the rabbi was in his hermitage. 'The rabbi is in the woods, the rabbi is in the woods again,' they would whisper to each other. As he agonised over the imminent death of his order, it occurred to the abbot at one such time to visit the hermitage and ask the rabbi if by some possible chance he could offer any advice that might save the monastery.

The rabbi welcomed the abbot at his hut. But when the abbot explained the purpose of his visit, the rabbi could only commiserate with him. 'I know how it is,' he exclaimed. 'The spirit has gone out of the people. It is the same in my town. Almost no one comes to the synagogue any more.' So the old abbot and the old rabbi wept together. Then they read parts of the Torah and quietly spoke of deep things. The time came when the abbot had to leave. They embraced each other. 'It has been a wonderful thing that we should meet after all these years,' the abbot said, 'but I have still failed in my purpose for coming here. Is there nothing you can tell me, no piece of advice you can give me that would help me save my dying order?'

'No, I am sorry,' the rabbi responded. 'I have no advice to give. *The only thing I can tell you is that the Messiah is one of you.*'

When the abbot returned to the monastery his fellow monks gathered around him to ask, 'Well, what did the rabbi say?'

'He couldn't help,' the abbot answered. 'We just wept and read the Torah together. The only thing he did say, just as I was leaving – it was something cryptic – was that the Messiah is one of us. I don't know what he meant.'

In the days and weeks and months that followed, the old monks pondered this and wondered whether there was any possible significance to the rabbi's words. The Messiah is one of us? Could he possibly have meant one of us monks here at the monastery? If that's the case, which one? Do you suppose he meant the abbot? Yes, if he meant anyone, he probably meant Father Abbot. He has been our leader for more than a generation. On the other hand, he might have meant Brother Thomas. Certainly Brother Thomas is a holy man. Everyone knows that Thomas is a man of light. Certainly he could not have meant Brother Elred! Elred gets crotchety at times. But come to think of it, even though he is a thorn in people's sides, when you look back on it, Elred is virtually always right. Often very right. Maybe the rabbi did mean Brother Elred. But surely not Brother Philip. Philip is so passive, a real nobody. But then, almost mysteriously, he has a gift for somehow always being there when you need him. He just magically appears by your side. Maybe Philip is the Messiah. Of course the rabbi didn't mean me. He couldn't possibly have meant me. I'm just an ordinary person. Yet supposing he did? Suppose I am the Messiah? O God, not me. I couldn't be that much for You, could I?

As they contemplated in this manner, the old monks began to treat each other with extraordinary respect on the off-chance that one among them might be the Messiah. And on the off-chance that each monk himself might be the Messiah, they began to treat themselves with extraordinary respect.

Because the forest in which it was situated was beautiful, it so happened that people still occasionally came to visit the monastery to picnic on its tiny lawn, to wander along some of its paths, even now and then to go into the dilapidated chapel to meditate. As they did so, without even being conscious of it, they sensed this aura of extraordinary respect that now began to surround the five old monks and seemed to radiate out from them and permeate the atmosphere of the place. There was something strangely attractive, even compelling, about it. Hardly knowing why, they began to come back to the monastery more frequently to picnic, to play, to pray. They began to bring their friends to show them this special place. And their friends brought their friends.

Then it happened that some of the younger men who came to visit the monastery started to talk more and more with the old monks. After a while one asked if he could join them. Then another. And another. So within a few years the monastery had once again become a thriving order and, thanks to the rabbi's gift, a vibrant center of light and spirituality in the realm.

'The Rabbi's Gift', as told in *The Different Drum*, M. Scott Peck

Question
Why do you think this story has been used as a response to the question of the sinful Church?

SUMMARY CHART

1.	The Disturbing Gospel	1.	– The prophets – The Gospel call
2.	Giving a Soul to Modern Society	2.	– The Christian vision for humanity – The Christian vision for the world
3.	The Church: the Embodiment of Faith	3.	– Faith needs embodiment – Church as the visible form of the Christian vision – Church as the living witness of the Kingdom of God – The challenge of the institutional Church – Faith as practised in the Church
4.	Towards an understanding of Church	4.	– The Church's understanding of itself – The founding of the Church – Models of the Church: Community Herald Sacrament Servant Institution
5.	The Sinful Church		

Revision questions and exercises

1. 'Man has little needs and deeper needs. We have fallen into the mistake of living from our little needs till we have almost lost our deeper needs in a sort of madness.' Discuss.

2. Is faith possible without a Church? Explain.

3. Why do you think we find it difficult to see ourselves as Church?

CHAPTER 3

The Church: The Parable of God

> Many people today have great difficulty with the Church's teaching role. This chapter analyses why people have such difficulty. It also examines the Church's teaching role in terms of:
>
> 1. the need to express beliefs
> 2. the unifying power of stated beliefs
> 3. the purpose of dogmas and doctrines
> 4. the hierarchy of truths
> 5. the question of authority

Introduction

The Church's teaching role causes difficulty for many people today.

Consider these attitudes:

1. There are some who have become quite hostile to the Church and its teachings. They view the Church as conservative and authoritarian with a message which seeks to limit human freedom and happiness at every opportunity. For such people, the Church is the great 'killjoy'. Its teachings are invariably seen as negative, intrusive and opposed to what they perceive as progress and change. They would like the Church to confine its interest to what they see as religious matters. Thus the Church's involvement in education, health care, or any enterprise which has public funding, causes particular difficulty for them. At the level of society, they would like to see the complete separation of the

activities of Church and State. The cry 'Why should the Church tell me what to do?' sums up their reaction at a more personal level.

2. On the other hand, there are those who feel that the Church has 'gone soft'. To them, the Church since Vatican II appears less certain, less demanding and more liberal than in former times. Very often such people see the decline in Church practice, faith and morals as the result of the emphasis on personal conscience which, to them, seems characteristic of the post-Vatican II Church. They long for the certainty and clarity of a time when Church teaching was black and white and definite demands were made on people. Many of these people would like the Church to be more vocal. Some would like to see Church laws enshrined in the laws of the land.

3. Another group holds less definite views. As the European Values Survey (1994) reveals, they are selective in what they think the Church should speak out on. They are sometimes described as à la carte Catholics. They welcome and support the Church's pronouncements on issues like racial discrimination and Third World problems, but are less enthusiastic when the Church speaks on matters pertaining to personal morality, especially sexual morality. They are also selective about which dogmas of the Church they choose to believe in. Thus, in the Republic of Ireland, while 98 per cent of Catholics believe in God, only 54 per cent believe in Hell.

Table 2.15 Percentage holding traditional religious beliefs among Catholics, by country

	God	Life after death	A soul	The Devil	Hell	Sin	Resurrection of the dead	Heaven
	Percentage believing							
	%	%	%	%	%	%	%	%
France	82	48	63	27	24	57	39	43
Great Britain	89	67	87	60	60	87	61	75
West Germany	74	49	69	21	18	63	42	38
Italy	90	60	73	39	39	72	50	51
Spain	88	45	64	29	29	61	35	52
Portugal	94	39	72	28	29	76	43	64
Netherlands	91	46	73	18	12	54	37	46
Belgium	86	46	66	22	20	55	38	40
Northern Ireland	99	69	90	75	70	92	77	89
Republic of Ireland	98	80	87	54	52	86	72	88

Table 2.17 Views among Catholics regarding issues on which it is proper for the Church to speak out

Rank		Percentage considering it proper
1	Third World problems	94
2	Racial discrimination	84
3	Abortion	82
4	Euthanasia	80
5	Unemployment	78
6	Extra-marital affairs	73
7	Disarmament	68
8	Homosexuality	61
9	Ecology and environment issues	59
10	Government policy	36

4. There is another group of people who might be described as traditional Catholics. Belief in God has always been part of their lives. They find meaning and comfort in their faith. They see the Church as a guide to Christian living. They are less inclined to question Church teaching than the other groups. Rather, they look to the Church for advice on matters ranging from personal problems to how they might vote on a particular moral issue.

5. Another group of people is simply indifferent to Church teaching. Some are indifferent to religion in the first place. Others view religion as an entirely personal and private affair – a matter between themselves and God only. Thus they see no role for the Church and its teachings in their lives.

6. There is also a group which has glimpsed and shares something of the vision which inspires Church teaching. While not blind to the imperfections and sinfulness of the Church, these people have made Church teaching their own. Thus, Church teaching is not regarded as an imposition but as a way of spelling out what it means to be a Christian.

Question and exercise
1. Describe the kinds of people who might hold each of these views.
2. Do you agree with any of the attitudes described here? Explain.

A closer look

These varying attitudes shed some light on why many people have difficulty with Church teaching today, yet the real source of such difficulty lies somewhat deeper. The priest psychologist Henri Nouwen has identified a number of reasons why many people experience such difficulty.

1. **ANSWERS WITHOUT QUESTIONS**

   In order to bring any kind of message or teaching to people, there has to be some openness, some willingness to accept the message. The people for whom the message is intended must have some question, some need, some desire that the message seeks to address. Otherwise the message falls on deaf ears, for

   > …whenever an answer is given when there is no question, support is offered when there is no need, or an idea is given when there is no desire to know, the only possible effect can be irritation or plain indifference.
   > *Creative Ministry,* Henri Nouwen

In other words, whenever people are locked in a world of secondary needs, whenever they are closed to the way of life that is inspired by belief in God, they will be unmoved, indifferent or even hostile to the message of Christianity. 'Faith is the assurance of things hoped for, the conviction of things not seen.' (*Heb 11:1*)

2. **THE REDUNDANCY OF THE MESSAGE**

   The Church's message is the Gospel, the Good News, yet many today feel that there is no news in much of what they hear. Very few people expect the Church to say something new, something they did not already know. Indeed, they feel they can predict what the Church's position is going to be on any given issue, and are turned off before the Church even begins to speak. The story of Jesus, his life, death and resurrection, is the core of the Gospel message. 'You must love the Lord, your God, with all your heart, with all your soul, and with all your mind, and you must love your neighbour as yourself', has been repeated so often that it has lost its original impact and fails to evoke even the slightest response. Sometimes it is as if people have been overfed the Christian message.

   > They have heard it from the time of their earliest childhood and will continue to hear it until they are dead – unless, of course, they become so bored on the way that they refuse to place themselves any longer in a situation in which they will be exposed to this redundant information.
   > *Creative Ministry*

   > We have tested and tasted too much, lover–
   > Through a chink too wide there comes in no wonder.
   > 'Advent', Patrick Kavanagh

3. **THE FEARFULNESS OF THE MESSAGE**

Perhaps the most basic reason of all why people have difficulty with the Church's message and teachings has to do with the nature of the message itself. The core truth of the Gospel is disturbingly radical. It is the call to inaugurate a new way of life, to establish the kingdom of God on earth. This is a way of life which is often at variance with the way of the world, and with many people's priorities and values.

> Who likes to hear, for example, that the last will be first, if he happens to be first? And who wants to hear that those who are poor, who mourn, who are hungry, thirsty and persecuted are called happy, when he is wealthy, self-content, well-fed, praised for his good wines, and admired by all his friends? Who wants to hear that he has to love his enemies and pray for those who persecute him…?
> *Creative Ministry*

The message of the Gospel, which is the basis for the teachings of the Church, often fails to find a home in our hearts because it may well have consequences for our way of life. It takes great courage and a firm belief in the Christian vision of human life and destiny to allow the message of Christianity to disturb the peace of a cosy existence.

Language and experience: symbols and meaning

Added to these difficulties, there is the question of the relationship that exists between language and experience, between symbols and their meaning. Human beings depend on words and symbols to communicate their ideas, feelings and beliefs. Yet we often experience difficulty finding words to express what we really mean. This is particularly true when we are trying to communicate a complex idea or something that we have experienced very deeply. At moments of profound sorrow or of overwhelming joy, we often find ourselves at a loss for words. This is because the things most deeply felt and experienced are the things that are most difficult to communicate. Our experience and its meaning are always bigger and deeper than the words and symbols we use to express them. This is why Plato insisted

that he had never written anything really serious because such things cannot be expressed. The poet Margherita Guidacci expresses something of the same idea when she says that 'words fail when affection overwhelms them'. So, too, the existence of God, the awareness of the transcendent, cannot really be communicated – it must be experienced.

Reasoned arguments do not necessarily prove the existence of God. They may serve as pointers; they may open our minds to the question of God, but ultimate proof for the existence of God lies deep within the soul. Christianity can only be understood if it is lived. Moreover, the language used to describe the transcendent reality we call God will always fall short of really communicating who God is. God is always bigger, always more profound that our human ways of talking about him.

There is yet another difficulty in all our attempts to talk about God. We often experience the tiredness and the emptiness of words and symbols. The words don't match our experience – the symbols don't convey any meaning. They have become redundant. What do terms like 'salvation', 'redemption' and 'fullness of life' mean for people today? Who knows what experiences symbols like water, oil and light seek to evoke? The original experiences that gave rise to such words and symbols in the first place have disappeared. We are left with 'empty gongs' and 'clashing cymbals'. We have arrived at T. S. Eliot's Wasteland, with its broken images. Indeed, we might well ask, with him,

> What are the roots that clutch, what branches grow
> Out of this stony rubbish? Son of man,
> You cannot say or guess, for you know only
> A heap of broken images, where the sun beats
> And the dead tree gives no shelter, the cricket no relief,
> And the dry stone no sound of water.

How we may envy the disciples' experience of Jesus – the kind of experience that caused them to declare that 'Jesus is Lord', 'God is Love'; the kind of experience that prompted them to commit to writing in the Scriptures, all they knew and all they wanted others to know about this man whom they recognised as saviour; the kind of experience that led a man who had denied Jesus three times to die for him later in Rome. How powerful, how vibrant, must the Gospel, the Good News of Jesus, have appeared to those early Christians.

Exercise
1. Contemplate the words 'fullness of life'. In what context have you heard them before? What do the words mean to you?
2. Sometimes symbols can become so commonplace that they no longer provoke a response. What do the following symbols evoke in you?
    a. your school crest
    b. the national flag
    c. the crucifix on a coffin
    d. the sanctuary lamp
    e. a holy water font
    f. the Paschal Candle
    g. the Angelus Bell

Religion and its expression

Perhaps one of the greatest risks we encounter in seeking to present and, indeed, to live the Christian message, is the temptation to distort it, to reduce it to that with which we are comfortable, to that which we want it to mean. Walter Kasper is mindful of this when he says that 'There is nothing so dangerous as religion. It can congeal into legalism and ritualism.'

1. To reduce religion to **legalism** is to reduce the call of the Gospel (life in all its fullness) to the mere keeping of laws, to turn Christianity into a morality play, where right living becomes an end in itself. To see Jesus merely as a moral teacher, to view the Church only in terms of its proclamations of what constitutes right living, is to miss the point. The first message of the Gospel is that God so loved the world that he gave his only Son, who in turn announced the coming of his kingdom. Human salvation, the conquering of evil and death, ultimate human happiness, have now been made possible. That is why a certain way of life is called for. The Good News is that God first loved us and we respond with a certain way of life – not the other way round. Thus,

> …the primary work of the Church is to bear witness to a gospel of human salvation; and all its other concerns, including its concern with morality, are in aid of that witness.
>
> *Church, State, Morality and Law*, Patrick Hannon

For the Christian, right living is always the consequence of belief in a caring God who wants the best for each one of us, for, in the words of St Athanasius,

> God became man, so that man might become divine.
>
> *De Incarnatione Verbi*, 54

The New Testament presents Jesus as someone who was critical of any attempt to reduce religion to the keeping of laws. Stories like that of the Good Samaritan, the Pharisee and the tax collector, and the woman caught in adultery all seek to present *the call of Christianity as something that is much bigger than rule-keeping*. The real heresy in reducing religion to legalism lies in the idea that people can save themselves – that someone can earn the right to salvation by right living. The New Testament teaches that it is Jesus, the Son of God, who saves. Salvation is offered to us as a free gift. The moral life is our response to the primary invitation issued by Christ.

2. To reduce religion to **ritualism** is to separate the idea of celebration from that which inspires it. Thus ritual becomes an empty formula which is unpleasing to God. The Old Testament prophets are mindful of this.

The prophet Micah asks:
> 'With what shall I come before the Lord, and bow myself before God on high? Shall I come before him with burnt offerings, with calves a year old? Will the Lord be pleased with thousands of rams, with ten thousands of rivers of oil? Shall I give my first-born for my transgression, the fruit of my body for the sin of my soul? *Mi 6:6–7*

The prophet Amos presents a God who is angry with such practices:
> 'I hate, I despise your feasts, and I take no delight in your solemn assemblies. Even though you offer me your burnt offerings and cereal offerings, I will not accept them, and the peace offerings of your fatted beasts I will not look upon. Take away from me the noise of your songs; to the melody of your harps I will not listen. *Am 5:21–23*

Instead, this is what the Lord wants:
> He has told us what is good. What he requires of us is this: to do justice, and to love kindness, and to walk humbly with our God. *Mi 6:8*

The Church as teacher

1. THE NEED TO TELL

Despite the inadequacies of language, and the hollowness of empty symbols, human beings have always felt the need to express themselves, to relate to and to celebrate their experiences with other human beings. This is particularly true when they have good news. Imagine how difficult it would be to keep to yourself the news that you had won the lottery. There is an almost irresistible compulsion to go out and tell people, to have them share in your joy and celebrate with you. This is also true of major achievements. When a person passes an important exam, gives up smoking or loses weight, or when a team has a major victory in a match, there is often the urge to tell people how it was done. When people are convinced that something is worthwhile and good, they want to bring others along with them, to share in their awareness.

Such is the basic human urge that lies behind the Church's teaching role. One can imagine the sense of excitement that accompanied the realisation of the early Church, that this man Jesus was in fact the Son of God, that he had come to save humankind. They could not but proclaim such good news to others, explain what it meant and its implications for their way of life. Despite the passage of time, it is still this realisation, this firm belief, that prompts Church teaching today. It is what lies behind all the Church's attempts to formulate, to put language on and to teach the message of Christianity. This is why the Church cannot be a silent Church. Moreover, its message is not for itself only. It is for all of humankind, for
> The joy and hope, the grief and anguish of the people of our time, especially of those who are poor or afflicted in any way, are the joy and hope, the grief and anguish of the followers of Christ as well. Nothing that is genuinely human fails to find an echo in their hearts.
> *Gaudium et spes*, 2

From the very beginning, the Church saw itself as charged to proclaim the Good News. The disciples were very conscious of 'being sent'. St Peter reported in the Acts of the Apostles:
> You know the word which [God] sent to Israel, preaching the good news of peace by Jesus Christ (he is Lord of all), the word which was proclaimed throughout all Judaea, beginning from Galilee after the baptism which John preached: how God anointed Jesus of Nazareth with the Holy Spirit and with power; how he went about doing good and healing all that were oppressed by the devil, for God was with him. And we are witnesses to all that he did both in the country of the Jews and in Jerusalem. They put him to death by hanging him on a tree; but God raised him on the third day and made him manifest; not to all the people but to us who were chosen by God as witnesses, who ate and drank with him after he rose from the dead. And he commanded us to preach to the people, and to testify that he is the one ordained by God to be judge of the living and the dead. To him all the prophets bear witness that everyone who believes in him received forgiveness of sins through his name. *Ac 11:36-43*

> I have sent you to be a light for the Gentiles, so that all the world may be saved. *Ac 13:47*

St Matthew's Gospel records Jesus commanding the eleven to:
> 'Go therefore and make disciples of all nations, baptising them in the name of the Father and of the Son and of the Holy Spirit, teaching them to observe all that I have commanded you.' *Mt 28:19-20*

2. DOGMAS AND DOCTRINES

Church dogmas and doctrines exist because God has said something. He has proclaimed salvation for all humankind. All the Church's dogmas and doctrines are attempts to spell out the Christian vision that is the foundation of faith. They are not ends in themselves. They make sense only in the light of the central truth of Christianity. They cannot be understood in an isolated way. They are related to the centre. They act as signposts in guiding people towards the central truth:
> Dogmas are lights along the path of faith; they illuminate it and make it secure.
> *Catechism of the Catholic Church*, 89

All dogmas and doctrines aim to express and teach the Christian faith and preserve it for future generations. They are the Church's attempt, over and over again, to make sense of and put words on what is inherently believed in the human soul. Indeed, they will only make sense if the truth of faith has first found a home in the heart of the human person.

Dogmas, doctrines and formulations are necessary because human beings need to have words put on things. We are not content to presume or take for granted the meaning behind words. We need to hear the words themselves. In close relationships, for example, even when there is much evidence of affection, we still need to hear the words, 'I love you'. Words have the power to evoke a response. Think of how someone reacts, think of the feelings and emotions that are evoked when someone hears the words, 'I love you'. As Teresa of Avila observes,

Words lead to deeds… They prepare the soul, make it ready and move it to tenderness.

Words and symbols also have a unifying purpose. They help to spell out people's beliefs, the identity they share and the allegiances that bind them together. Think of the unifying effect of a national flag or anthem. Think of the reason for a school motto, a club mascot or a team jersey. Think of the reason behind a country's constitution, or why any organisation or group of people feel the need to put together, often in writing, what they believe fundamentally. It is no coincidence that the first attempt by the early Church to state its position formally was prompted by the issue of Gentiles becoming Christians. Up to this time, the followers of Jesus had been Jews, and now Christians were faced with the question of who they were and who could belong to their community.

Since that first meeting at the Council of Jerusalem, the Church has met time and time again to consider the Christian vision in the light of the Church's experience of living in the world. Believing itself to be guided by the Holy Spirit, and faithful to the word of Scripture and the wisdom of tradition, the Church seeks to address all new questions in the light of its central belief. Thus, for instance, when the Church today considers twentieth-century questions like nuclear war, surrogate motherhood or in vitro fertilisation, its guiding principle is how such practices fit in with its understanding of human nature in accordance with God's plan. The Church professes two truths about the human person – that human life is both sacred and social.

> Because we esteem human life as sacred, we have a duty to protect and foster it at all stages of development, from conception to death, and in all circumstances. Because we acknowledge that human life is also social, we must develop the kind of societal environment that protects and fosters its development.
> *Consistent Ethic of Life,* ed. T. Fuechtmann

3. THE HIERARCHY OF TRUTHS

In the *Decree on Ecumenism,* Vatican II speaks about a hierarchy of truths.
When comparing doctrines with one another, they should remember that in Catholic doctrine, there exists an order or 'hierarchy' of truths, since they vary in their relation to the foundation of the Christian faith.

What Vatican II is recognising here is that, while all doctrines seek to make faith clear, some are more central to the essence of faith than others. It is not that some doctrines are irrelevant or need not be believed; it is, rather, that some doctrines, some truths, are based on others which have a higher priority. These doctrines, what we might call 'secondary truths', are a spelling out of a primary or fundamental truth:

> The Mystery of the Most Holy Trinity is the central mystery of Christian faith and life. It is the mystery of God in himself. It is therefore the source of all the other mysteries of faith, the light that enlightens them. It is the most fundamental and essential teaching in the 'hierarchy of the truths of faith'.
> *Cathechism of the Catholic Church,* 234

4. THE AUTHORITY OF THE CHURCH

For most people the word 'authority' has negative connotations. When we think about somebody in authority, we think about somebody whose role it is to impose certain ways of behaviour on us, to limit our freedom and, ultimately, to judge and inflict penalties on us. Thus the notion of coercion or force is often built into our understanding of authority.

Yet the word 'authority' has much more positive origins. It is derived from two Latin words, *auctor,* meaning 'creator' or 'author', and *auctio,* meaning 'growth'. Some of this more positive understanding of authority has survived to today. For example, we speak about somebody being an authority on art or antiques and so we look to them for advice. We talk about somebody like Nelson Mandela enjoying great authority among his people. The implication here is that such a person has certain qualities that others admire and freely allow themselves to be influenced by. There is a sense of respect and trust between such people. Such a person is looked to for guidance and direction, because he or she is seen to have an in-depth knowledge or understanding of or an insight into that which others value. Thus when we say that someone 'speaks with authority' we are saying that that person has the vision and conviction that makes a leader. We automatically respect and are influenced by those whom we know speak the truth and practise what is right. This is because the

> …most basic of all authority is the authority of truth or right. When we can see for ourselves that something is true or right, we can make it the author of our life-style.
> *Problems of Religious Faith,* J. P. Mackey

The New Testament presents Jesus as someone who spoke with authority. It was his knowledge, his intimacy with the Father that gave him such authority. Later the question 'Who do you say that I am?' was addressed to those who knew Jesus best. The authority of the Church, therefore, is the authority of the Gospels.

> The one sent by the Lord does not speak and act on his own authority, but by virtue of Christ's authority…. From him, they receive the mission and the faculty ('the sacred power') to act *in persona Christi Capitis.*
> *Catechism of the Catholic Church,* 875

It is the Church's unique insight into the person and mission of Jesus Christ which is the basis for what we call the authority of the Church. It does not exist to badger us into belief. Rather it exists as a source of guidance for all of those who wish to find the truth.

Conclusion: the Church — The parable of God

As teacher, Jesus made frequent use of parables. Through his parables he revealed the truth about human life and destiny as envisaged in the Kingdom of God. The parables reveal the kind of attitude and priorities that are part of this Kingdom. They issue an invitation to the hearer to come and see, to risk surface living in order to live more deeply. Jesus himself might well be described as the 'parable of God', in that in him this invitation was made flesh. Continuing the work of Jesus, the Church might be described as the 'parable of God'.

> As Church, we form a counter-culture to our world, but a counter-culture of a most ironic sort. We seek not to coerce and badger our neighbours, but to live our lives of intimacy in trusting openness to them, always hoping that they may see in us something of the 'parable of God', and finally get the point of it all.
> *Redemptive Intimacy,* Dick Westley

The Church is called not simply to preach the Good News but also to live it. This is the only way in which it can really be the Church of Christ. It is the only way, too, in which it can be the Church of the world, for

> Modern man listens more willingly to witnesses than to teachers, and if he does listen to teachers, it is because they are witnesses.
> *Evangelii nuntiandi*

	SUMMARY CHART		

1. Problems with Church Teaching

    1. Answers without questions
   - the redundancy of the message
   - the fearfulness of the message
   - the limitations of language
   - empty words and symbols
   - the dangers of legalism and ritualism

2. The Church as Teacher

    2. The need to tell
   - dogmas and doctrines
   - identity and unity
   - the hierarchy of truths
   - the authority of the Church

Revision questions and exercises

1. Write an essay entitled 'The Church in Ireland today'.

2. Imagine that you are a member of the hierarchy about to explain the Church's teaching on a particular issue. Name the issue and write the explanation you would give.

3. 'Modern man listens more willingly to witnesses than to teachers, and if he does listen to teachers, it is because they are witnesses.' Discuss.

CHAPTER 4

Introduction to Morality

> This chapter asks how people arrive at moral decisions. It suggests that behind each moral decision lies a certain philosophy or vision of life. It considers other influences on our moral decisions and actions – needs, emotions, fears, personality. It also discusses the sources of morality, our peer-groups, our emotions, the State and, finally, the natural law, which is the ultimate or eternal law that is written on human hearts.

Introduction: A pluralist society

The following story was told by a Jesuit priest writing in an American publication. A class was invited to consider a typical moral dilemma that might be faced by a young woman. This was the ensuing dialogue:

> Teacher: 'So those are the choices open to her. What should she do?'
>
> Students: 'It's her choice.'
>
> Teacher: 'Yes, we know it's her choice. But how should she choose? and on what grounds?'
>
> Students: 'It's her choice.'
>
> *Understanding Veritatis Splendor*, ed. John Wilkins

This exchange illustrates an attitude towards the making of moral decisions with which many people identify. This attitude is born out of the emphasis on human freedom which is very much part of a *pluralist* society, where people are presented with many options. There is often little agreement on what is the right thing to do because external sources of authority or objective moral teachings are seen as an intrusion on human freedom. This is why the students resist giving the woman advice, insisting, instead, that 'it's her choice'.

Exercise
HOW PLURALIST IS THIS CLASS?
1. Survey the views of the class on the following issues:
   a. Not paying tax is all right if you can get away with it.
   b. Pre-marital sex is all right if two people love each other.
   c. Abortion is always wrong.
   d. Lying to protect a friend's reputation is right.
   e. It is the common good that counts, not the individual's rights.
   f. Using the office phone for personal calls is all right because everyone does it.
   g. We should not give to the Third World – we have enough poor at home.
   h. It is the State's job to look after Travellers.
2. List/categorise the range of views expressed in your class. How varied are they?
3. Do certain views dominate? Why do you think this is so?
4. Is it easy to hold a minority viewpoint? Why/Why not?

How do people arrive at moral decisions?

On the one hand, in a pluralist society individual freedom is regarded as important. On the other hand, if we examine how the young woman in the story eventually arrived at the decision, or if we look at the factors that influenced our views in the exercise, it is clear that nobody arrives at a decision completely free of all influence, i.e. morally neutral. Our past experiences, the society in which we live, our understanding of ourselves, of others and of the world, all influence the views we hold and the decisions we make. In other words, a certain philosophy or understanding of life underpins all the moral decisions we make.

Consider these philosophies, each of which illustrates a certain view of the meaning and purpose of life.

1. Pragmatism
is not concerned about the rightness or wrongness of an action in itself but rather with what works in a given situation. It is very much concerned with the real world and the here and now.

2. Hedonism
corresponds to the 'playboy' theory of life. The pleasure principle, especially physical and sensual, dominates this philosophy. There is little reference to the consequences of actions in this philosophy except where they might affect the perpetrator.

3. Humanism
values humanity for its own sake. Actions are either right or wrong depending on their effect on other people.

4. Atheistic existentialism
is a very individualistic way of looking at humanity. Its most famous advocate was the French philosopher, Jean-Paul Sartre, who believed that every person is radically alone and separated from others.

5. Religion
Those who approach life from a religious point of view regard actions done in this life not only as good or bad in terms of how they affect other people, but also as reflecting a belief in ultimate or eternal life.

6. Agnosticism
accepts that there is a certain lack of direction or purpose to our actions. Nothing is seen as ultimately good or ultimately bad. What I think today is all that counts.

7. Communism
believes that the individual has value only to the extent that he or she contributes to the welfare of the State.

8. Materialism
sees the acquisition of material things as the recipe for human happiness.

Exercise

1. Examine each of the statements below. Which philosophy of life does each one reflect?

    'Whatever works is right. People or things are worthwhile as long as they are useful.'

    'We're here for one purpose: to get as much enjoyment out of life as we can. Pain and suffering are evils to be avoided at all costs. The main thing in life is always to feel good.'

    'Human beings have value. Therefore, we should be concerned for our fellow human beings all over the world.'

    'Freedom is the most important thing. Freedom means doing what I want to do. Hell is other people. What is good is that which furthers my interests.'

    'The ultimate meaning of life is to be found in God. Everything we do is a search for God and the happiness he offers to the human race.'

    'Live for today; who knows what the future may bring.'

    'The individual has no worth. What is important is the group. The individual's purpose in life is to work for the glorification of the group.'

    'More money, a nicer home, a bigger car. These are the only values worth living for.'

2. Which of the philosophies described above is closest to your own?

3. Examine your own life to date. Who or what has influenced you most?

Other influences

Needs, emotions, fears: While it is true that people act out of their particular philosophies of life, other factors also play a role in their decisions. Human needs, emotions and fears often influence how we act. Even laziness can be a factor! Thus, for example, people may choose not to drink and drive, not because they are convinced that it is wrong in itself but because they fear the consequences. A pupil may lie for another pupil because he fears that he will be bullied if he doesn't. A person may need the approval of others, so she does something, for example publicly giving to charity, to win such approval, not because the deed is good in itself. Somebody else might do something to go along with the crowd, even though she knows the action is wrong, because she doesn't want to stand out. At times, parents may not want to upset their children or simply haven't time to spend with them, and so they give in to them and allow them to eat sweets or watch television or stay out late, even though they may know that this is taking the easy way out. A teenaged couple wants to sleep together because each has strong feelings for the other. They act because it 'feels right'.

Personality: Personality type may also affect moral decisions. Some people are naturally rebellious. They do not want to accept the status quo and they particularly resent things being imposed on them. Sometimes they just want to be awkward or different. Sometimes they are simply looking for notice.

Other people are conformists. They go along with the majority view because it is the easiest thing to do. Their reasoning is 'it must be okay if everyone is doing it'. They are often unwilling or unable to reason things out for themselves. Essentially, they do not want to be different.

Then there are the legalists. They like things to be black and white, and clearly spelled out in rules and regulations. Their idea of right behaviour is keeping to the letter of the law. They are very uncomfortable with complex issues or so-called 'grey areas' which may be difficult to spell out in law.

Then, there are the thinkers. They use reason to decide on actions or issues. They consider all the factors involved and the possible consequences. They are willing or even anxious to consult others, but ultimately they make up their own minds.

Sources of morality

We get our first ideas about what is right and wrong from those around us:

1. THE HOME: As children our first awareness of what is right and wrong comes from our parents in the home. Here we are presented with moral directives like 'it is wrong to steal', 'it is good that you should share your toys', 'it is right to tell the truth'. Such influence is crucial in developing our moral outlook or sense of right and wrong. However, as we grow older, we are less inclined to accept the moral ideas of others without question. This is part of growing up. It is natural for a child to accept without question what is presented by its elders. It is not natural or desirable for an adult to do so. Moreover, as we grow up we discover that there is not always agreement amongst our elders about what is right and wrong. Sometimes we have to reject what has been presented because we discover for ourselves that it is wrong. Thus, while we are all influenced by our homes and our backgrounds, growing up enables us to be more than mere products of our environment. We can question it and make it our own, which sometimes means rejecting the values we have been given.

2. PEER GROUPS: We have already seen that part of growing up involves challenging and questioning what was given to us as children. Sometimes, however, we reject our parents' ideas, not because we discover that they are flawed, but, rather, because as teenagers we are challenging them as sources of authority in our lives. We want to be free of their influence. Often we replace this source of authority with that of our friends or peer group. At this time in our lives our friends have a huge influence on us and on the decisions we make. Yet it would be a mistake to think that our friends are always right, and it is a sign of immaturity blindly to accept their ideas about right and wrong. Growing up involves coming to our own understanding of what is right and wrong.

3. EMOTIONS: Young people often rely on emotions to make moral decisions. We cannot dismiss the power or role of emotions in helping us to make good decisions. It is often feelings of concern, of sympathy or of love which move us to good actions. On the other hand, it would be a mistake to let feelings or emotions be the sole determinants of our actions. At times our emotions can be irrational and can cloud our thinking, causing us to act in a way in which we might not normally act, or in a way that is not ultimately good for ourselves or for others.

4. THE STATE: For many people the State is the ultimate source of morality. If something is wrong in the eyes of the State they accept it as being wrong in itself. Much of the time the ideas of right and wrong as understood by the State and as enshrined in its laws are in keeping with what is actually right and wrong. Yet it would be a mistake to accept without question the State as the absolute source of right and wrong. Most people in the civilised world accept that the ideas of right and wrong as understood by the Nazi regime were seriously flawed. Yet many Germans accepted them without question. Rudolf Hoess, Commandant of Auschwitz, described his reaction when he was ordered to organise the mass extermination of the Jews:

Pope John Paul II at Auschwitz

It was certainly an extraordinary and monstrous order. Nevertheless, the reasons behind the extermination programme seemed to me right. I did not reflect on it at the time: I had been given an order and I had to carry it out. Whether this mass extermination of the Jews was necessary or not was something on which I could not allow myself to form an opinion, for I lacked the necessary breadth of view. If the Führer himself had given the order for the 'final solution of the Jewish question', then, for a veteran National Socialist and even more so for an SS officer, there could be no question of considering its merits. 'The Führer commands, we follow' was never a mere phrase or slogan. It was meant in bitter earnest.

After the war, Albert Speer, Hitler's Minister of Armaments and War Production, said that he considered himself guilty of the murder of millions of Jews at Auschwitz even though he did not know about it:

> One day, some time in the summer of 1944, my friend Karl Hanke, the Gauleiter of Lower Silesia, came to see me. In early years he had told me a great deal about the Polish and French campaigns, had spoken of the dead and wounded, the pain and agonies, and in talking about these things had shown himself a man of sympathy and directness. This time, sitting in the green leather easy chair in my office, he seemed confused and spoke falteringly, with many breaks. He advised me never to accept an invitation to inspect a concentration camp in Upper Silesia. Never, under any circumstances. He had seen something there which he was not permitted to describe and, moreover, could not describe.
>
> I did not query him, I did not query Himmler, I did not query Hitler. I did not speak with personal friends. I did not investigate – for I did not want to know what was happening there. Hanke must have been speaking of Auschwitz. During those few seconds, while Hanke was warning me, the whole responsibility had become a reality again. Those seconds were uppermost in my mind when I stated to the international court at the Nuremberg Trial that as an important member of the leadership of the Reich, I had to share the total responsibility for all that had happened. For from that moment on, I was inescapably contaminated morally; from fear of discovering something which might have made me turn from my course, I had closed my eyes. This deliberate blindness outweighs whatever good I may have done or tried to do in the last period of the war. Those activities shrink to nothing in the face of it. Because I failed at that time, I still feel, to this day, responsible for Auschwitz in a wholly personal sense.

Nazi Germany was a totalitarian state, yet even in democratic countries there are people who take their ideas of right and wrong from the State. If the State permits abortion or euthanasia there is a number of people who believe that such actions are right because the State says so. Some people allow the State to be their conscience and to decide what is right and wrong for them; it is their way of avoiding mature moral thinking and the responsibility for their actions.

Other people expect the State to reflect through its laws all their own beliefs about right and wrong. This is neither possible nor desirable. How, for instance, could the State make laws dictating that people should be kind or charitable? These are desirable moral actions but they cannot be enshrined in law.

> It is easy to see that adultery is incompatible with a belief in the value of fidelity in marriage, but it does not follow that it should be punished by the law of the land.
> *Church, State, Morality and Law*

Morality is always bigger than that which can be legislated for.

5. **THE NATURAL LAW:** We have just seen that parents, friends, our emotions, and even the State cannot serve as absolute sources of morality for us. The idea that there is an ultimate or eternal law which is above human law is an ancient one, and is found in many traditions. We see it in Sophocles' play *Antigone* which was written in Greece four hundred years before Christ.

In the play, Antigone is determined to bury her dead brother Polynices, even though King Creon has ordered that his body be left unburied as a punishment for his rebellion. Antigone is brought before the King and argues that in burying her brother she is following a higher law than that of the King:

> King Creon: Now, tell me... Did you know the order forbidding such an act?
>
> Antigone: I knew it, naturally. It was plain enough.
>
> King Creon: And yet you dared to contravene it?
>
> Antigone: Yes. That order did not come from God. Justice, that dwells with the gods below, knows no such law. I did not think your edicts strong enough to overrule the unwritten unalterable laws of God and heaven, you being only a man. They are not of yesterday or today, but everlasting; though where they came from, none of us can tell.

Here Antigone displays an innate sense of the rightness of the decision to bury her brother despite the King's law. Something deep within her convinces her of this. This inner sense of rightness is sometimes called the moral law or the natural law, because it is found within human nature itself. When we study human nature

> we gradually come to perceive more clearly what actions are good and what are evil. It is something we can only do slowly and with many mistakes along the way. We need the help of what other and wiser people have said. Even after deep thought and study we can disagree with one another over certain moral questions. But basically we can say what is natural is good, that is, it is good if it fits in with man's nature as a person and as a member of the human race; and it is bad if it does not.
> *The Moral Life*

Throughout history various attempts have been made to spell out what is meant by the moral or natural law. This is usually done by listing rights or duties. Thus, in 1776 the American Declaration of Independence said:

> We hold these truths to be self-evident: that all men are created equal; that they are endowed by their creator with certain inalienable rights; that among these are life, liberty and the pursuit of happiness.

In 1948, the United Nations drew up the Universal Declaration of Human Rights. The Ten Commandments list those duties which are founded on the moral or natural law. In all of these declarations and commandments there is much agreement on what constitutes good and bad behaviour.

Exercise
1. Which of the sources of morality presented here has the most influence on you at your present stage in life?
2. Which source of morality do you think has the most influence on the majority of people today?
3. Which source of morality impresses you most? Why?
4. If what is natural is good,
    a. What actions do you think are natural and therefore good?
    b. What actions might be considered unnatural and therefore bad?

TOWARDS AN UNDERSTANDING OF MORALITY

The medieval philosopher Thomas Aquinas (1225-74) summed up morality in one sentence: 'Good must be done and evil must be avoided.' While most people will agree with this statement the difficulty is in deciding what is good. Even if we agree that what is natural is good, a difficulty arises when what is good for me is not good for another person. For example, it is good that I should enjoy playing music; but what if the playing of my music disturbs somebody else's sleep or their concentration on work? It is good that I should marry; but what if the person I want to marry is already married to someone else?

The sources of morality we have just considered are attempts to spell out the rights and duties of human beings. Philosophers, too, have attempted to formulate the moral principle which seeks to protect my rights as well as those of the other person:

> Act only according to the maxim which you can at the same time will to be a universal law.
> Immanuel Kant, 1724–1804

Immanuel Kant

Here is an example of what Kant means:
> Say I am tempted to lie or to steal, because it would suit me to tell this lie or steal this article. Before I go ahead, I should stop and think what would happen if this were made into a general rule that applied to everyone else. If everyone lied or stole whenever it suited them, no one could ever be believed and no one could ever be trusted. That shows, says Kant, that lying and stealing are wrong – and they are wrong for me as well as for everyone else.
> *The Moral Life*

CHAPTER 5

What Is Truth?

> Give me truths, for I am weary of surfaces and die of inanition.
> *Ralph Waldo Emerson*
>
> At a time when people are offered a variety of options where human behaviour is concerned this chapter asks 'What is truth?' It acknowledges that the human search for truth goes back to the time of the early Greek philosophers. It presents the Christian vision of morality as being founded on the truth about human nature and destiny as understood in the light of God.

Introduction: pluralism, freedom and moral relativism

> Life is now a smorgasbord with an endless array of options. Whether a hobby, holiday, life-style, world-view or religion, there's something for everybody.... Putting it simply, we have reached the stage in pluralisation where choice is not just a state of affairs, it is a state of mind... change becomes the very essence of life.
> *The Gravedigger File*, Os Guinness

The world as described by Os Guinness is a world of choice. It is a world which emphasises human freedom and the individual's right to make decisions. Thus, in chapter 4, 'It's her choice', was the only advice offered to the young woman about to make her decision.

At first glance, this attitude towards the woman's decision seems very attractive. It is allowing her to be free; it is respecting her right to choose. Such an attitude appears modern, tolerant and mature. Yet we might ask ourselves what position we might hold, how neutral we might be, if she were about to steal our bike or harm someone close to us? Could we maintain our disinterested position? Would we want to allow her such freedom and, if not, why not?

Questions like these raise doubts about the absolute emphasis we sometimes place on individual human freedom. On the one hand there is much that is good about the modern emphasis on human freedom. Pope John Paul II acknowledges this in his encyclical, *Veritatis splendor.*

> Certainly people today have a particularly strong sense of freedom… 'the dignity of the human person is a concern of which people of our time are becoming increasingly more aware'. Hence the insistent demand that people be permitted to 'enjoy the use of their own responsible judgment and freedom, and decide on their actions on grounds of duty and conscience, without external pressure or coercion…'. This heightened sense of the dignity of the human person and of his or her uniqueness, and of the respect due to the journey of conscience certainly represents one of the positive achievements of modern culture. *VS,* 31

On the other hand, to make human freedom an absolute value over and above all other values is to create a situation where 'each individual is faced with his own truth different from that of others'. (*VS,* 32). In this context there is no objective truth – no universal agreement on what is good and what is evil. We construct our own values, our own morality. There is no shared vision, no common understanding, no united belief about what constitutes right and wrong. Everything is *relative.*

To be truly able to say that 'it's her choice' implies that the decision she makes is of no consequence to me. Is it of no consequence to me if she is about to cheat in a State examination, sell a few Ecstasy tablets to her friends or drive a car without insurance? To leave moral choices to the individual and to adopt a neutral stance is to relegate morality to the private domain. To do this, however, is to make a statement about what we consider to be of value, what we consider worth publicly defending. Thus,

> By relegating the decision over euthanasia, for example, to the private wishes of individuals, government is declaring that the life of the sick and dying is of no inherent value.
> *After Ideology,* David Walsh

Morality becomes a matter of personal feeling and expression, relative to an individual or group of people at a specific time and place and context. In this context, human life, whether it be that of the unborn or of the dying, only has the value that the individual may or may not choose to give it.

Yet, however prevalent this attitude may be today, it can be difficult to live with. Sooner or later, a situation arises which causes people to seek objective standards of behaviour. The 'back to basics' mentality, the rise in fundamentalism, the public demand to teach about right and wrong following the killing of Jamie Bulger, all represent a certain dissatisfaction with moral relativism as the most effective way of living together. Even in the United States, pluralist since its very foundations, free from the close link between Church and State that was the experience of much of Europe, the last decade has seen the re-opening of the abortion debate, an issue many believed was settled in 1973 when abortion became legal.

Perhaps this rethink is because:
> A private morality is no more possible than a private language.
> *The Persistence of Faith*, J. Sacks

Perhaps, too, it is because we occasionally sense something of what we have in common as human beings.

> …mortal beings, facing the mystery of death, beings with aspirations to peace and truth and beauty which this world seems incapable of satisfying, beings who, however tossed around by events, know that we are somehow called to be faithful to our commitments, that it is nobler to die than to violate our dignity or that of any fellow human being.
> *Life in All Its Fullness*

Exercise
1. What does it mean to say that 'a private morality is no more possible than a private language'?
2. Do you think the question of euthanasia should be decided by governments? What moral issues do you think should be publicly defended? Why do you think it is possible to reach agreement on those things that should be publicly defended?
3. 'Each individual is faced with his own truth, different from that of others.' What things do you hold to be true? How different is your idea of truth from that of the rest of your class?

The search for truth

PHILOSOPHY AND THE SEARCH FOR TRUTH

The search for truth and the question of how life should be lived have occupied the minds of some of the greatest thinkers in the world. Western philosophy began 2,500 years ago when the Greeks sought the truth about the world as they experienced it. The great preoccupation of the early Greek philosophers was the problem of the One and the Many. If, they asked, everything in the world is changing all the time, is it possible to find any underlying order, any permanent reality behind the changing appearances of the world? **Heraclitus** argued that the only permanent feature of the world was that everything changes all the time. 'The world is always in a state of flux.' **Parmenides**, on the other hand, argued that the world was formed from some unchanging substance – something permanent. However, the only truth that can be discovered about this permanence is simply that it is. Nothing more can be said about it. A third Greek philosopher, **Democritus**, put forward what might be called a compromise theory. He believed that the world was made out of single, indivisible units called atoms. The form and shape of each atom cannot change but atoms are constantly moving and rearranging themselves. Thus there is both a permanent and a changing aspect to the universe.

The Allegory of the Cave

These early Greek philosophers were concerned about truth and the question of change in the physical world. Later philosophers like Socrates and Plato were concerned with the truth about how life should be lived – ethical or moral truth, as opposed to scientific truth. This story is taken from Plato's *Republic*.

> People are sitting in a cave, facing the wall at the back of the cave, their faces turned away from the cave opening and the sunlight. There is a fire outside the cave but all the people can see are the flickering shadows on the wall of those who are passing outside. To them, the shadows are the real thing. They mistake the shadows for reality. Imagine then if one of the prisoners were suddenly set free. Initially he would be blinded by the light outside when he confronted reality. Gradually, however, he would become accustomed to the light and would see things as they really are. Then he would return to the cave to tell the others the truth of what he saw.
> 'The Allegory of the Cave'

Socrates believed that if a person knew the right thing, then he or she would do it. No one does wrong willingly. He was deeply concerned with the difference between opinion (what I think is right) and truth (what I know is correct). Opinion changes, truth is fixed. Socrates' great insight was that knowledge is truth. His pupil, Plato, shared this belief:

> When the mind's eye is fixed on objects illuminated by truth and reality, it understands and knows them, and its possession of intelligence is evident: but when it is fixed on the twilight world of change and decay, it can only form opinions, its vision is confused and its opinions shifting, and it seems to lack intelligence.
> *The Republic*

PLATO'S IDEA OF FORMS

Plato believed that the world was divided into reality and appearance – knowledge (truth) and opinion – the One and the Many. We seek knowledge or truth but opinion is usually all that we have, though it may pass for knowledge. This is because people focus on the visible world – the world of the senses, rather than on an intangible world – a world beyond the senses, a world of true knowledge. Thus, for example, a person may be concerned with beautiful things – things which he or she considers beautiful. But this is a matter of opinion. Someone else may not consider these things beautiful. The person who is concerned with the higher world, the world of true knowledge, is concerned with beauty itself. There are particular instances of beauty in the physical world, in the world of the senses, but they all share in what Plato called the universal form of beauty. The same can be said about truth and justice and, ultimately, about the Good which Plato saw as the supreme form. The Good – the Agathon – is the highest form of knowledge. It is from the Good that all the virtues and all the forms of knowledge are derived and it is towards the Good that the soul reaches. The movement towards this highest form – the Good – is the true measure of right action: everything that leads towards it is good, while everything that distracts from it is bad. This is the essential moral vision of Plato, four hundred years before the time of Christ.

Exercise

1. Why do you think some of the greatest thinkers in the world have been obsessed with the question of truth? Are we less concerned with this question today? Explain.

2. Reflect on Plato's allegory of the cave. Have you ever had the experience of being convinced by something because you had a moment of insight?

3. Do you believe that there is such a thing as absolute truth, absolute beauty, absolute goodness? Why? Why not?

THE CHRISTIAN MORAL VISION

> Christians, recognise your dignity and, now that you share in God's nature, do not return to your former base condition by sinning. Remember who is your head and of whose body you are a member. Never forget that you have been rescued from the power of darkness and brought into the light of the Kingdom of God.
>
> *Sermo 21,* St Leo the Great

Much of people's difficulty with moral teaching and, perhaps, especially with Church teaching on morality, stems from their perception that morality is about rules to be followed – rules devised and handed down by a source of authority which seeks to coerce and badger people and limit their freedom. The debates on issues like contraception, abortion and divorce all bear witness to this perception. Yet the real source of conflict is not so much about different views on a particular moral issue, but, rather, the failure to understand the vision of human life and destiny that gives rise to such views in the first place. Without knowing, without sharing this vision, it is difficult to avoid experiencing Church teaching as an imposition.

THE SPLENDOUR OF THE TRUTH

In his encyclical *Veritatis splendor* (The Splendour of the Truth), Pope John Paul II sets out the vision which has inspired all Christian moral teaching for the last two thousand years. The encyclical opens with the question put by the rich young man to Jesus in Matthew's Gospel. This is his search for truth.

> 'Teacher, what good deed must I do, to have eternal life?' *19:16*

Jesus' response is:

> 'Why do you ask me about what is good? One there is who is good. If you wish to enter life, keep the commandments.' He said to him, 'Which?' And Jesus said, 'You shall not kill; you shall not steal; you shall not bear false witness; honour your father and mother; and, you shall love your neighbour as yourself.' The young man said to him, 'All these I have observed: what do I still lack?' Jesus said to him, 'If you would be perfect, go, sell what you possess and give the money to the poor, and you will have treasure in heaven; and come, follow me.' *19:17-21*

At one level, this is a story of a man who approaches Jesus and questions him about morality: 'Teacher, what must I do...?' However, as Pope John Paul II points out, the real question for the young man is not so much about rules to be followed, but about the real meaning of life (*VS*, 7): 'What must I do to have eternal life?' This is the question, the hope that lies at the heart of every human decision and action. What will make us happy? Nobody does something that he or she feels will bring unhappiness. Thus the main point of the story of the rich young man is that there is a connection between moral good and human destiny and fulfilment. It is therefore not so much a question of what I must do to fulfil the law, but, rather, what must I do to be ultimately happy?

Something of the same idea is found in Dostoyevsky's story 'The Dream of a Ridiculous Man'. This man has begun to feel that 'everywhere in the world, nothing matters'. He comes home one evening determined to commit suicide. Before he reaches home, however, he meets a young girl who pleads for his help. He brushes her aside but cannot get her out of his mind. Her suffering touched him; he has discovered that something does matter. He falls asleep and begins to dream. In the dream he has been shot and is inside a coffin being buried. He prays for help. Suddenly, he is lifted up and travels through space until he reaches the fabulous setting of the Greek islands. This is paradise. It is filled with beautiful 'children of the sun', living in perfect harmony with one another and with nature. 'Innocent gladness sounded in the words and voices of these men.' After a while he notices a change in them. They have become corrupt, lost their innocence, are now given over to anger, jealousy, cruelty and lies. It dawns on him that he has been responsible for their contamination. 'The point is that I have... debauched them all.' He is like the bad apple which has rotted all the others.

Fyodor Dostoyevsky

When he wakes up, he no longer wants to kill himself. Instead he wants to plunge himself into life. He now wants to give himself over to the truth he discovered in his dream, where 'ecstasy, immeasurable ecstasy lifted my whole being'. He has discovered that right living is the key to happiness. The great truth is that to be happy one has only to turn away from evil.

I refuse and am unable to believe that evil is a normal condition in men. Yet they laugh at this belief of mine. But how can I help but have faith: I saw Truth – my mind did not invent it, and I saw it, saw it and its image filled my soul forever...

What must we do to be happy?
The main thing is – love thy neighbour as thyself: This is the cardinal point; that's all, and nothing further is needed; it would at once be discovered how things should be arranged.
  The Diary of a Writer, Fyodor Dostoyevsky

 **Exercise**
1. Examine Dostoyevsky's story, 'The Dream of a Ridiculous Man'. Why does this man feel suicidal? What kind of a life do you think he has been living? Why does he no longer want to kill himself after his dream?

2. What is your understanding of fulfilment? What do you think would make you ultimately happy?

3. Do you really think there is a connection between our moral life – the way we treat others – and our own ultimate happiness?

SEEING THE LIGHT

> Yet they laugh at this belief of mine.

The title of Dostoyevsky's story is 'The Dream of a Ridiculous Man'. This man appears ridiculous to those on the outside, those who, like the prisoners in Plato's cave, have not yet seen the vision of the Good. We are often in the same situation when we view the Christian call to morality from the outside. It seems ridiculous: its commands are felt as impositions rather than as the natural outcome of seeing the Truth. The Christian vision of morality is about the promise of ultimate human fulfilment.

> …not morality, but fulfilment. And there is no fulfilment other than that of love, meaning the renunciation of self and dying to the world…. To dissolve oneself in love. It will be the power of love that creates, rather than myself. To lose oneself. To deny oneself in the fulfilment and passion of Truth.
> *Notebooks II*, Albert Camus

This is why the final words of Jesus to the rich young man are:
> 'If you would be perfect, go, sell what you possess and give the money to the poor, and you will have treasure in heaven; and come, follow me.' *Mt 19:21*

To discover this truth for oneself is a lifelong journey. It is a journey that will lead to many falls and many attempts to turn back. The way of superficiality, the way of appearances will always tempt us. Yet, in our better moments we know that this is the only journey worth taking. It is the only journey that does justice to our dignity and nature as human beings. This is because

> All humans desire to participate in what is ultimately meaningful and enduring rather than to lose or dissipate themselves in what is passing and senseless.
> *After Ideology*

Those who have seen the light, those who have glimpsed the truth, cannot help but utter the words of the Italian poet, Margherita Guidacci:

And still I tell you: 'Persevere.'
Whether you have come shipwrecked by a harsh
storm of the Sirtis, or undertook your journey voluntarily
in this inhospitable expanse, persevere, traveller,
to the very end, though you have
no other guide but your anxiety
and dismay. Truth awaits man, but awaits him only
when his last step has been taken.

    'Libyan Sibyl', from *A Book of Sibyls*

Libyan Sibyl by Michelangelo, Sistine Chapel

CHRISTIAN MORALITY

For the Christian, Jesus Christ is the one who has realised the truth in himself. In him the truth about the ultimate goodness of God and the human capacity to reach perfect fulfilment in this goodness was achieved. Moral action, therefore, for the rest of humanity becomes a matter of following his example, of, in the words of St Paul, 'putting on the mind of Christ'. Thus, Christian morality is not primarily about rules. It is about living in a way that reflects and respects the dignity of all human beings.

> Moral rules have no other function than to foster and protect the truth and the humanity of our lives and relationships.
> *Can These Bones Live?*

Group work
1. Consider the moral issues listed on p. 71.

2. Outline the arguments for and against each issue.

3. What is the underlying vision or understanding of human nature in each set of arguments?

POSSIBLE VISIONS

1. God is the author of human life. Only God can decide when it should end. Human life is always sacred.

2. People can decide in certain circumstances when it is permissible to take human life.

3. People have a right to their own happiness.

4. People deserve a second chance at happiness.

5. A promise is a promise – it should always be kept.

6. It is wrong to use other people for our own happiness.

7. Pleasure is the most important thing in life.

8. What matters is not getting caught.

Moral Issue	Arguments in Favour	Arguments Against
Abortion	1. The woman has the right to choose.	1. No one has the right to take another human life.
	2. It is better to have an abortion than to have a baby without a father.	2. However difficult the circumstances, they do not justify taking the life of the unborn.
	3. To go through with the pregnancy would cause major difficulty for the woman.	3. To attack the unborn is to attack the innocent and the vulnerable.
	Vision: The mother's right to life and to happiness has a prior right over that of the foetus.	Vision: All human life is sacred, from the moment of conception.
Euthanasia	1	1
	2	2
	3	3
	Vision	Vision
Divorce	1	1
	2	2
	3	3
	Vision	Vision
Sex outside marriage	1	1
	2	2
	3	3
	Vision	Vision
War	1	1
	2	2
	3	3
	Vision	Vision

CHAPTER 6

The Call of Conscience

> This chapter examines the question of conscience and law. It highlights the importance of the exercise of conscience and the necessity for an informed conscience. It analyses the difference between a sincere and a truthful conscience and, finally, it discusses the purpose of law.

Introduction

Conscience is the most secret core and sanctuary of a man. There he is alone with God whose voice echoes in his depths.
The Church in the Modern World, 16

To act from one's conscience is to act from within oneself – to decide from within one's own heart what action one is going to take. Conscience is the witness of what takes place in the heart of a person. It is the only witness because what takes place in the human heart is hidden from the eyes of everyone outside. VS, 57

Consider the following situations:

Situation A

You have borrowed your father's car without permission. You had to get to town and you have no other way of getting there. Everything goes fine until you are pulling out of a parking space and you reverse into the car behind you. You have done no damage to your father's car but the door of the other car is badly dented. You look around; nobody has seen what has happened. It is easy to drive away. Your father would be furious if he knew you took the car and you're not even insured.

What do you do?

Situation B

Christmas is coming and you have very little money to buy presents for your family. You have no part-time job this year because you have to study for your exams. You are walking down town and you find a wallet. When you open it you discover that it belongs to a neighbour of yours and there is £200 in it. You know your neighbour has plenty of money and, after all, you would spend the money buying presents for your family and not on yourself.

What do you do?

Situation C

You have been told to wait in the Principal's office. On the desk you see the maths exam he has prepared for your class next week. You find maths difficult and there's a lot of pressure on you to do well. Moreover you have missed a number of classes because you were sick, and that wasn't your fault. If only you knew what was coming up… and it would make your parents very happy.

What do you do?

Exercise
1. What did you decide to do in each of these situations?
2. How did you arrive at your decision?

Conscience

Conscience has been described as the self making a moral judgement. Sometimes, as you may have discovered in the exercise, people arrive at a moral judgement by thinking and reasoning – taking into account all the factors involved, maybe even consulting others and then making up their own minds. Most of the time, however, people act from habit, sometimes from a good habit, sometimes from a bad habit, and little time is spent deciding what course of action should be taken. Upbringing, education, the law and maybe even religious principles have made us the kind of people we are and we act accordingly. At other times we may experience conscience in a much more obvious way, when we find ourselves in a dilemma about how to act.

CONSCIENCE IN ACTION

Conscience determines the kind of characters we have, the kind of people we become. To act in conscience is to be true to ourselves – to act in character. Thus we sometimes speak of people acting out of character when something they do is not in keeping with their normal actions. One of the most vivid illustrations of living in accordance with one's conscience is found in Robert Bolt's play *A Man for All Seasons*, which tells the story of Sir Thomas More.

Sir Thomas More and his household, engraving by Hans Holbein

Thomas More is Chancellor of England and a friend of King Henry VIII. Henry wants to divorce his wife Catherine and marry Ann Boleyn because he wants a male heir. The Pope refuses to give him permission so he declares himself head of the Church in England. Thomas More does not support the King's actions. In this scene with the Duke of Norfolk, he defends his loyalty to the Pope:

Norfolk: All right – we're at war with the Pope! The Pope's a Prince, isn't he?

More: He is.

Norfolk: And a bad one?

More: Bad enough. But the theory is that he's also the Vicar of God, the descendant of St Peter, our only link with Christ.

Norfolk: *(sneering)* A tenuous link.

More: Oh, tenuous indeed.

Norfolk: *(To the others)* Does this make sense? *(No reply; they look at More.)* You'll forfeit all you've got – which includes the respect of your country – for a theory?

More: (*hotly*) The Apostolic Succession of the Pope is (*stops; interested*) …Why, it's a theory, yes; you can't see it; can't touch it; it's a theory. (*to Norfolk, very rapidly but calmly*) But what matters to me is not whether it's true or not but that I believe it to be true, or rather, not that I *believe* it, that *I* believe it…

Later, once again speaking to the Duke of Norfolk about his refusal to sign the Act of Succession, he says:

More: And what would you do with a water spaniel that was afraid of water? You'd hang it! Well, as a spaniel is to water, so is a man to his own self. I will not give in because I oppose it – I do – not my pride, not my spleen, nor any other of my appetites but, *I* do – *I*.

Norfolk tries to persuade Thomas More to take the oath. After all, everyone else has taken it:

Norfolk: I'm not a scholar, as Master Cromwell [the prosecutor] never tires of pointing out, and frankly I don't know whether the marriage was lawful or not. But damn it, Thomas, look at those names…. You know those men! Can't you do what I did, and come with us, for fellowship?

More: (*moved*) And when we stand before God, and you are sent to Paradise for doing according to your conscience, and I am damned for doing according to mine, will you come with me, for fellowship?

Cranmer: So those of us whose names are there are damned, Sir Thomas?

More: I don't know, Your Grace. I have no window to look into another man's conscience. I condemn no one.

Finally, when in prison in the Tower of London, Thomas More's daughter, Margaret, arrives to try to persuade her father one last time to swear to the Act:

More: You want me to swear to the Act of Succession?

Margaret: God more regards the thoughts of the heart than the words of the mouth. Or so you've always told me.

More: Yes.

Margaret: Then say the words of the oath and in your heart think otherwise.

More: What is an oath then but words we say to God?

Margaret: That's very neat.

More: Do you mean it isn't true?

Margaret: No, it's true.

More: Then it's a poor argument to call it 'neat', Meg. When a man takes an oath, Meg, he's holding his own self in his own hands. Like water. (*he cups his hands*) And if he opens his fingers then – he needn't hope to find himself again. Some men aren't capable of this, but I'd be loath to think your father one of them.

Exercise
1. Examine the reasons given by Thomas More for not swearing to the Act of Succession. What understanding of conscience do they demonstrate?

King Henry VIII

Sincere and truthful conscience

To follow one's conscience is a moral imperative. Ultimately, we can only be true to our own nature, we can only be at peace with ourselves if we follow our conscience, for

> He who acts against his conscience loses his soul.
> *Fourth Lateran Council,* 1215

That is not to say that conscience is always right. With the best will in the world our moral judgements can be mistaken. We see examples of this every time people quarrel, every time they go to court, every time countries go to war. Each side claims to be acting for the good, but both sides cannot be right. Somebody must be wrong. This is what is meant by the difference between a sincere and a truthful conscience. In other words, what I believe to be the truth about a particular situation may not in fact be the truth. Sincerity cannot make what is intrinsically a bad action good.

An extreme example of this can be seen in the case of Jack the Ripper. Apparently he claimed that in acting as he did he sincerely believed that he was acting for the good of society, ridding it of the evil of prostitution. Yet, we would argue that in fact – in truth, what he did was not right. The motivation may have been sincere, but the action was wrong.

At the same time, it is possible for a person to carry out a good deed for the wrong reason. To give to the Third World, for example, is a good deed. Yet I am not acting from a sincere conscience if my principal motivation is to get tax relief, or to impress others. Indeed, as Thomas à Becket puts it in T. S. Eliot's play, *Murder in the Cathedral*:

> The last temptation is the greatest treason:
> to do the right deed for the wrong reason.

For an action to be truly right it should come about as the result of sincere and truthful conscience. Thus if I give to the Third World because I want to help people less well-off than myself, then I am acting from a right motive and I am doing the correct thing.

RATIONALISING

At times we are very good at justifying or defending our own actions. As was shown in the exercises at the beginning of the chapter, we can think of any number of reasons for justifying the things that we do. We call this *rationalising*. This means that we are either blind to the truth, or we do not want to see it. Others may see the truth but we convince ourselves of the rightness of our actions. In Gilbert and Sullivan's *Princess Ida,* the spiteful King Gama suggests that he is trying to help others by his nasty remarks:

> If you give me your attention, I will tell you what I am:
> I'm a genuine philanthropist – all other kinds are sham.
> Each little fault of temper and each social defect
> In my erring fellow-creatures I endeavour to correct.
> To all their little weaknesses I open people's eyes,
> And little plans to snub the self-sufficient I devise;
> I love my fellow creatures, I do all the good I can.
> Yet everybody says I am such a disagreeable man:
> And I can't think why!

Another way of rationalising is to make the excuse that 'everyone is doing it'. At the back of our minds we know that a certain action is wrong but we want to continue with that action, so we try to excuse our conduct by hiding behind the decisions of others.

Exercise
1. Give examples of people acting out of the different levels of conscience.

2. Have you ever tried to justify something when deep down you knew it was wrong? Explain.

The Church and conscience

The Church has always defended the primacy and dignity of conscience:

Thomas Aquinas
> Anyone upon whom the ecclesiastical authority, in ignorance of the true facts, imposes a demand that offends against his clear conscience, should perish in excommunication rather than violate his conscience.
> *IV SENT,* d. 38, 1.4

John Henry Newman
> Certainly, if I am obliged to bring religion into after-dinner toasts (which indeed does not seem quite the thing), I shall drink – to the Pope, if you please – still to conscience first, and to the Pope afterwards.
> *Letter to the Duke of Norfolk*

Vatican II
> In all his activity a man is bound to follow his conscience faithfully, in order that he may come to God, for whom he was created. It follows that he is not to be forced to act in a manner contrary to his conscience. Nor, on the other hand, is he to be restrained from acting in accordance with his conscience, especially in matters religious.
> *Declaration on Religious Freedom,* 3

> In the depths of his conscience, man detects a law which he does not impose upon himself, but which holds him to obedience. Always summoning him to love good and avoid evil, the voice of conscience can when necessary speak to his heart more specifically: do this, shun that. For man has in his heart a law written by God. To obey it is the very dignity of man; according to it he will be judged. Conscience is the most secret core and sanctuary of a man. There he is alone with God, whose voice echoes in his depths.
> *Pastoral Constitution on the Church in the Modern World,* 16

John Henry Newman

John Paul II
> The Church puts herself always and only at the service of conscience, helping it to avoid being tossed to and fro by every word of doctrine proposed by human deceit, and helping it not to swerve from the truth about the good of man, but rather, especially in more difficult questions, to attain the truth with certainty and to abide in it.
> *Veritatis splendor,* 64

We get a glimpse of what the Church means by conscience in the statements we have just considered. Essentially the Church identifies three dimensions to conscience:

1. *Conscience is the basic orientation in us towards what is good.* It follows from what we call the moral law or the natural law. It is what St Paul describes as the law that is written in the human heart (*Rm 2:14-15*).

2. *Conscience must be informed.* However, 'Conscience as the judgement of an act is not exempt from the possibility of error… Conscience is not an infallible judge; it can make mistakes.' That is why, 'in order to have a 'good conscience' (*I Tm 1:5*), man must seek the truth and make judgements in accordance with that same truth.' (*VS*, 62)

FORMING ONE'S CONSCIENCE

We have already seen the difference between a sincere and a truthful conscience. We have also acknowledged how easy it is for us to rationalise and convince ourselves that something is good. This second dimension of conscience is concerned with the judgement of conscience as based on the truth. An old rhyme poses many of the questions we must ask ourselves as we seek the truth:

I keep six honest serving men.
They taught me all I know.
Their names are What and Why and When
And How and Where and Who.

These are the questions we must bring to any situation to enable us to decide upon the right action. The most important question is What? Is what I am about to do good or bad in itself? The question Why? concerns my motivation. The questions When? How? Where? and Who? concern the circumstances surrounding a situation which may make a normally good act bad.

As human beings seeking to act in a moral way – seeking the truth and thus seeking to inform our consciences – we can consult our own experience as well as that of our family, our friends, experts in the field and society at large. As Christians we have access to the wisdom of Scripture and the Church's teaching.

We need to do this because:
Only through dialogue with many sources of moral wisdom do we come to know what it means to be human in a truly moral way.
To Walk Together Again, Richard M. Gula

In his book *How Do I Know That I Am Doing Right?*, Gerard Sloyan lists the following things which enable us to inform our consciences and bring us closer to the truth of our actions:

- *Have a pure intention.* Sincerity is important. A person who wants to do something simply 'to get away with it' hardly has what might be considered a pure intention. The following questions help us to discern a 'pure intention': Why do I want to do this? Is my motivation selfish? Is it for the sake of others? Will this action benefit me, that is, help me to grow? Have I considered all the data? Am I acting on impulse?

- *Consult the teaching of Jesus in the New Testament, of the Prophets, Moses and Paul.* If I really want to be a Christian, that is, a follower of Jesus Christ, I must know what he said and reflect seriously on its meaning as well as I can. Am I aware, for example, of the 'ethical teachings of Jesus'? The Ten Commandments? The position of the Church?

- *Ask the question: 'How does this action of mine measure up to the yardstick of love?'* For the Christian, every authentic response to God and neighbour is a response in love. And love is not something watered down but a real, self-sacrificing attempt to meet others and God. Is my concept of love more than just 'feeling'? Do I realise that love consists in giving as well as receiving?

- *Consult the people of God wherein Christ and his Spirit reside.* What is the teaching and belief of the bishops, theologians, holy and learned men, the brotherhood of believers? Do I even care what this teaching is? Do I consult it? Do I bother asking other Christians for an opinion?

- *Follow the current debate on the great moral issues.* For example, what are the pros and cons with regard to abortion, mercy-killing, premarital sex? Particularly, what is the position of the Catholic community on these issues?

- *Pray for God's graceful guidance in all my actions.* Ask God's Spirit to make me a creature of love. If I sincerely want to do the right thing, I should follow the above directives, and ask for God's help; he won't mislead me. Doing the right thing with God's help brings calmness and peacefulness.

- *Be sorrowful for my sinfulness, not just my sins, confessing them fully and humbly, asking for the help of God.* Sure, there are times when we are going to fail. At times, we forget who we are, that we are God's children. There are times when immediate gratification, what others think, even laziness, help influence us to make a wrong decision. But God understands that. He simply wants us to admit that we have failed to live as his children. Like the father in the parable of the Prodigal Son, he is always willing to claim us as his own and shower his abundant love on us. All we need to do is turn back to him and ask for his help.

- *Follow 'my' conscience.* When all is said and done, I must follow my conscience.

3. *The third dimension of conscience is the actual moral judgement we make in a given situation.* It is the judgement that is right for me. As we saw with Thomas More it is not the judgement of what someone else must do – it is only what *I* must do.

THE PURPOSE OF LAW

Generally speaking the idea of law does not enjoy popular press. We associate law with rules and regulations which we interpret as limitations on our freedom. Who, for instance, is overjoyed by the concept of school rules and regulations! At the same time we often associate law with hypocrisy. We remember the Pharisees in the New Testament who were so concerned with observing the letter of the law that they had lost sight of its spirit. The danger with law is that it can too easily be reduced to legalism, which is the bare minimum of morality.

In an ideal world laws would be unnecessary. People would be so mindful of the rights of others that they would never act in a way which would infringe those rights. However, life is far from ideal and people are far from perfect. Thus law, whether civil or Church, seeks to protect human rights and guide human behaviour. It is born out of the accumulated wisdom of those who have gone before us. The law of the land, the Ten Commandments, the precepts of the Church all represent attempts to protect the basic minimum requirements of those who live in society or who belong to the Church. It is impossible, however, to legislate for concern or kindness or love, those more positive qualities which make society more human and which lie at the heart of Christianity.

Of course there can be bad laws. Thomas Aquinas put forward the following characteristics of good law:

1. It must be reasonable.

2. It must be for the common good.

3. It must be made by a competent authority.

4. It must be promulgated [made known].

Exercise
1. Devise a rule or law for your school or society, keeping in mind Aquinas' requirements for good law.

2. 'A morality of rules is a minimum morality' (Donal Murray). What do you think this statement means?

CHAPTER 7

The Sacrament of Reconciliation

Introduction

No other sacrament has suffered the same decline in participation as has the Sacrament of Reconciliation. While the level of Mass attendance, especially in this country, remains high (80 per cent still attend on a regular basis), there is no corresponding level of attendance at the Sacrament of Reconciliation. This is the case even though, as every child knows, First Communion is preceded by First Confession.

On closer observation, however, the decline in numbers attending the sacrament may tell us more about our overall approach to faith than about our high level of participation in the other sacraments. In this country it is easier to 'opt into' sacraments like Baptism, Confirmation, Eucharist and Marriage than it is to opt out of them. There are all sorts of pressures on people to get married in church, to have their children baptised and make their First Holy Communion and Confirmation. In a culture where this is the norm in most schools, it requires determination for people to have their children opt out of these sacraments. Thus the high levels of participation may sometimes be more the result of cultural and social factors than statements about commitment in faith. Very often it may be that people simply go along with the crowd where these sacraments are concerned.

On the other hand, it is interesting to note that the one sacrament that demands an individual and personal response has shown the greatest decline. While, as we have observed, it is easier to opt into some of the other sacraments than it is to opt out of them, participation in the Sacrament of Reconciliation is very much a conscious decision. It involves examining our own lives and having an awareness of a sense of sin.

Exercise
1. Would you want to get married in church? Why/Why not?
2. Would you have your children baptised and participate in the other sacraments? Why/Why not?

Why have the numbers decreased?

There are many reasons for the decline in participation in the Sacrament of Reconciliation.

1. In the past our sense of sin was linked with ideas about rules that had been broken, an authority that had been disobeyed and a God who would punish. Fear of hell and damnation played a major part in people's understanding of sin and sometimes they were forcefully reminded of it, as the poet, Francis Harvey, and the story-teller, Frank O'Connor, recount:

   ### The Redemptorists of My Youth

   They had one-track minds and
   declamatory hands; they were
   superb actors in a dying or dead
   tradition not unaware of
   the dramatic impact of a black
   biretta flourished above a bowed head.
   They strode like soldiers into
   embattled pulpits and wore
   crucifixes like swords
   at their waists. Their invocations were
   trumpet calls to battle against
   the world, the flesh and the devil
   and each flickering candle in our hands was
   a faggot lit to burn another heretic. They flushed
   sin from the coverts of our souls with
   fear and drove God's sacred plover crying
   into the upland rain where it remains.
       Francis Harvey

   Then, to crown my misfortunes, I had to make my first confession and communion. It was an old woman called Ryan who prepared us for these. She was about the one age with Gran; she was well-to-do, lived in a big house on Montenotte, wore a black cloak and bonnet, and came every day to school at three o'clock when we should have been going home, and talked to us of Hell. She may have mentioned the other place as well, but that could only have been by accident, for Hell had the first place in her heart.

   She lit a candle, took out a new half–crown, and offered it to the first boy who would hold one finger – only one finger! – in the flame for five minutes by the school clock. Being always very ambitious I was tempted to volunteer, but I thought it might look greedy. Then she asked were we afraid of holding one finger – only one finger! – in a

> little candle flame for five minutes and not afraid of burning all over in roasting hot furnaces for all eternity. 'All eternity! Just think of that! A whole lifetime goes by and it's nothing, not even a drop in the ocean of your sufferings.' The woman was really interesting about Hell, but my attention was all fixed on the half-crown. At the end of the lesson she put it back in her purse. It was a great disappointment; a religious woman like that, you wouldn't think she'd bother about a thing like a half-crown.
> 'First Confession', Frank O'Connor

2. Today people see themselves as more enlightened and more sophisticated than the people of Harvey's youth or O'Connor's imagination. They view such an understanding of sin and of the authority of the Church as the product of another age. Some of them smile at what they see as the innocence and immaturity of a time past. Others bear resentment towards a Church which, as they see it, brought fear and guilt into people's lives. For this reason they want to dissociate themselves from the Church and, particularly, from the Sacrament of Reconciliation.

> The Sacrament of Reconciliation makes no sense without an awareness of sin. Modern society does not foster such an awareness. Instead there is a strong bias against negative feelings and self-evaluations. People are encouraged to think positively, to develop self-esteem and to become confident. The 'think big', 'you can do it', 'go for it' mentality which we sometimes associate with American culture has become part of our culture too. Moreover, as one theologian notes, there is the strong emphasis on competition which carries with it the need for self-promotion based on deeply-rooted convictions that one 'deserves' to be promoted and to accumulate goods, power and status at others' expense.
> *Sign of Reconciliation & Conversion,* Monica Hellwig

Such was the theme of the film *Wall Street,* which sought to make a virtue out of profit, big business and self-advancement. Michael Douglas' declaration that 'greed is good' summarises the key belief of this kind of society. Such a belief hardly fosters a sense of sin.

3. Allied with the 'feel-good' factor is a new attitude towards guilt. Some people feel that even the worst criminals should not be blamed or punished for their actions. Rather they should be seen as sick people, victims of circumstance, and therefore should be diagnosed, treated and rehabilitated rather than made to feel guilty and punished. People often argue that hereditary and environmental factors have more to do with people's wrongdoing than any deliberate, free decision on their part.

> Side by side with its exaltation of freedom, yet oddly in contrast with it, modern culture radically questions the very existence of this freedom. A number of disciplines, grouped under the name of the 'behavioural sciences', have rightly drawn attention to the many kinds of psychological and social conditioning which influence the exercise of human freedom…. But some people, going beyond the conclusions which can be legitimately drawn from these observations, have come to question, or even deny, the very reality of human freedom.
> *VS,* 33

Sigmund Freud

Psychiatrists tell of the high percentage of patients who suffer from neurotic guilt, which has a very negative influence on their lives and general mental health. Sigmund Freud developed the idea of the *super-ego* as a way of understanding the reason why people often experience such guilt. Freud believed that psychotic patients often suffer from the delusion of being watched. They feel that people are waiting for them to do something wrong so that they can be punished. This is because there is a self above the normal self – a super-ego which judges the self. This super-ego is formed when we are children – we absorb the attitudes, rules, judgements and punishments that we experience at home and in school, and from other sources of authority, including the Church. These are external sources of authority, outside judges of our behaviour. However, we internalise or make their judgement or message our own as we grow older. In this way, the super-ego replaces our early authority figures. The more we have been judged, condemned and made to feel guilty as children, the more our super-ego will make us feel guilty as adults.

There is a strong reaction today against those things which could induce such feelings of guilt. However, in the attempt to remove those things which cause unnecessary and unhealthy guilt, people sometimes create the impression that it is wrong to feel any guilt at all. Without a sense of guilt, without the experience, the realisation that we have done wrong, the Sacrament of Reconciliation serves no purpose.

4. Even when people do become aware of wrongdoing, either in their personal lives or as members of society, they are more inclined to look to sources of reconciliation other than the sacrament itself. Thus when people become aware of hatred, envy, jealousy or other resentments in their lives, they turn to a psychoanalyst. If there is tension or fighting in the family they tend to seek the intervention of a marriage counsellor. If they realise the extent of the injustices in society, they may join organisations, discussion groups or action groups where they can share their concerns and propose certain forms of action. Even if they are looking for Christian conversion in their lives, they are more likely to join a prayer group or Bible study class than to avail of the Sacrament of Reconciliation. If they are worried about matters of conscience, like birth control, they are more likely to discuss it with someone who has had a similar experience than to bring their question to the priest in Confession.

5. For many people, too, their alienation from the Sacrament of Reconciliation stems from the sacrament itself as they have experienced it. Many people tell stories of a bad experience with a cranky or insensitive priest. 'That's me done with Confession', is a frequent reaction!

Other people may not have had this experience but still feel a quiet dissatisfaction with their experience of the sacrament. Sometimes the sacrament seems empty and shallow in comparison with the depth and complexity of the concerns, questions and feelings which they bring to it. Real-life situations and experiences are rarely black and white. A rushed confession of broken rules, or a list of sins committed, rarely does justice to what lies at the heart of such wrongdoing. When this is the case, the person often leaves the confessional feeling empty and somewhat disappointed. They do not feel that they have been uplifted or freed from the distress or anxiety which prompted their confession in the first place.

Sometimes, too, there is the failure to understand the role of the priest in the Sacrament of Reconciliation. Even when people do have a sense of sin, they talk about confessing directly to God, and 'cutting out the middle-man'.

6. Finally, there is a general superficiality and distraction attached to modern living which

pushes the questions of God and the Christian lifestyle into the background. To paraphrase Vatican II, some never get to the point of raising questions about God or where they stand in relation to him, since they neither experience religious stirrings nor sense why they should trouble themselves about such questions. Such people are often closed to the depth dimension in life. They are carried along by the tide of modern living. They understand what it means to break the law, but not what it means to sin. They rarely stop to examine the meaning of life or where they are going. The Sacrament of Reconciliation, which demands such an examination, is simply irrelevant to them.

For reflection
1. Can you remember the last time that you felt a personal sense of wrongdoing or guilt?
2. What has been your experience of the Sacrament of Reconciliation?
3. Do you feel the need for this sacrament in your life now? Why/Why not?

Why the sense of sin has been lost

Perhaps the most significant factor affecting our attitude towards the Sacrament of Reconciliation is the loss of a sense of sin in modern society. In part, this is a reaction to the over-emphasis on sin in the past. Such things as 'smoking, drinking, the popular election of judges, the country fair, horse racing, cock-fighting, dining at men's clubs and enjoying oneself on the Sabbath by swimming, sliding and skating' (Benjamin Rush, 1788) were all condemned as sins. For a priest to celebrate Mass without wearing a biretta was considered a venial sin. There were so many rules to be followed that it was almost impossible not to be in a constant state of sin. Sometimes, the result of this preoccupation with rules is a dismissal of all ideas of sin.

A mistaken idea of conscience has also affected our sense of sin. Many people confuse conscience with doing as they please without any reference to outside guidance or authority.

> 'What is right' very easily becomes 'what I like' and since there is no strong urge to do what one dislikes, the lines between right and wrong become blurred, moral conflict disappears, and with it the whole notion of sin.
> *Has Sin Changed?* Seán Fagan

There is sometimes a denial of or a refusal to face up to sin. The very language we use in describing actions often illustrates this. Thus we describe abortion as 'the termination of pregnancy'; wiping out thousands of innocent lives as 'ethnic cleansing'; telling lies as 'being economical with the truth'; embezzlement as 'creative accounting'. Such a refusal to name our actions and to face up to their seriousness is found in William Golding's *Lord of the Flies*. A young boy, Simon, has been killed by his schoolmates who have now turned into a barbaric mob. Afterwards Ralph and Piggy are talking. Ralph is deeply upset by what has happened. He is shocked by the deed that has been carried out. Piggy, on the other hand, tries to deny and make excuses for what has happened:

At last Ralph stopped. He was shivering.

'Piggy.'

'Uh?'

'That was Simon.'

'You said that before.'

'Piggy.'

'Uh?'

'That was murder.'

'You stop it!" said Piggy, shrilly. 'What good're you doing talking like that?'

He jumped to his feet and stood over Ralph.

'It was dark. There was that – that bloody dance. There was lightning and thunder and rain. We was scared!'

'I wasn't scared,' said Ralph slowly, 'I was – I don't know what I was.'

'We was scared!' said Piggy excitedly. 'Anything might have happened. It wasn't – what you said.'

He was gesticulating, searching for a formula.

'Oh Piggy!'

Ralph's voice, low and stricken, stopped Piggy's gestures. He bent down and waited. Ralph, cradling the conch, rocked himself to and fro.

'Don't you understand, Piggy? The things we did – '

'He may still be – '

'No.'

'P'raps he was only pretending – '

Piggy's voice tailed off at the sight of Ralph's face.

'You were outside. Outside the circle. You never really came in. Didn't you see what we – what they did?'

There was loathing, and at the same time a kind of feverish excitement in his voice.

'Didn't you see, Piggy?'

'Not all that well. I only got one eye now. You ought to know that, Ralph.'

Ralph continued to rock to and fro.

'It was an accident,' said Piggy suddenly, 'that's what it was. An accident.'

His voice shrilled again.

'Coming in the dark – he had no business crawling like that out of the dark. He was batty. He asked for it.' He gesticulated widely again.

'It was an accident.'

'You didn't see what they did – '

'Look, Ralph. We got to forget this. We can't do no good thinking about it, see?'

'I'm frightened. Of us. I want to go home. O God I want to go home.'

Mass production, the scientific and technological revolutions have made life more comfortable for many. The emphasis on human rights today can make us feel that cruelty, barbarism and injustice are characteristics of former times. We sometimes forget that the dream has not come true for everyone, that living conditions in ghettos and slums are often worse today than ever before, that the old are often lonelier than they were in times past, and that with modern technology we have discovered even more cruel ways of killing one another.

On the other hand, we sometimes feel that there is so much evil in the world, that there are so many evil people, that we ourselves are not so bad relatively speaking. It is easy to gloss over our own sense of sin when we feel that there are others worse than we are. This is one symptom of our refusal to face up to sin in ourselves. We tend to make excuses for ourselves very easily, to justify what we have done. 'Anybody else would have done it if he were in my shoes.' 'It was the woman you put with me; she gave me the fruit and I ate it' (Gn 3: 12). Even when we do sense that we have done wrong we are often unwilling to face up to the consequences. We may want to be free from whatever guilt we experience, but we are unwilling to confess to or to undo the wrong which has caused our guilt in the first place. We want 'to cease being guilty and yet not to make the effort of cleansing ourselves' (Albert Camus). To live in a kind of a 'limbo', not too guilt-ridden and yet not uplifted and freed from the source of our guilt, sometimes seems to be all we want today.

Question
Some commentators argue that modern living has numbed our awareness of a sense of sin. Do you agree? Is it a good or a bad thing?

Sin, repentance, forgiveness, reconciliation

In order to understand what sin really means, one must begin by understanding that God is leading us, and the universe he created, to a goal.
The Inner Truth, Donal Murray

The Christian understanding of sin is based on God's ultimate plan for us. It is based on the idea that ultimate human happiness can only result from a life that is oriented towards God and the well-being of our fellow human beings. Sin in this context is viewed as the condition or state where we are not tuned into or turned towards this plan which God has for humankind. Thus both the Old and New Testaments and various theologians in the Church describe sin as:

— the lack of something which ought to exist;
— turning away from the direction in which one should be going;
— 'missing the mark';
— acting as if I were the only one who counted;
— seeking to finding meaning in life without reference to God.

This understanding of sin is less about rules to be followed and more about *what direction my life is taking.* Theologians sometimes called this idea the **'fundamental option'** which indicates what kind of people we have chosen to be, what kind of lives we have chosen to live. It is the overall direction our lives are taking. This should not be thought of as something separate from individual actions or choices. Our choices both express and shape what we are. Unjust actions make an unjust person. Sin in this sense is essentially about the person. It is more than a crime – it is more than breaking the law. It is a breach of a relationship which we should have with God and with humanity. We can best understand what is meant here if we analyse how human relationships work. In a relationship that is good, people naturally act in a certain way. They value the relationship, give time to it and, generally speaking, behave in a way that fosters it. Occasionally they may do things or, indeed, fail to do things, the outcome of which has a negative effect on the relationship. Such actions or omissions are out of tune with the general way the relationship is going. If the relationship is to survive it must be realised that wrong has been done and there must be an attempt to come to the senses and so restore the relationship to what it once was.

THE STORY OF THE PRODIGAL SON

Perhaps the best illustration of this understanding of sin and, indeed, of repentance, forgiveness and reconciliation, is found in the story of the Prodigal Son (*Lk 15:11-32*). The following reflection on this story is given by the theologian, Monica Hellwig:

> The sinner is represented as having travelled away from home, away from the father, having squandered his inheritance until finally he realises that he is terribly alienated in a utterly inauthentic and unsatisfying existence. An aspect of the parable that is very interesting is that according to the property laws and inheritance customs of the time the younger son had done something illicit though not at all unusual. By the Hebrew law the father could convey the ownership of the younger son's one-third share of inheritance during his lifetime but with all sorts of safeguards to prevent its being sold or the income from it being spent against the father's approval. Nevertheless, at the times when emigration seemed an attractive alternative to the poverty of Palestine, it was not unknown for sons to want and obtain their inheritance in cash and emigrate to cities of the diaspora [the dispersed communities of Jews who lived outside the Holy Land].
>
>
>
> Several facts are of great interest in the analogy from contemporary life that Jesus chose in order to make his point. The issue is one of independence – not of freedom so much as of independence. According to the traditional law it was an illegitimate independence that undermined life according to the covenant. The father of the story, like the actual fathers of the time, nevertheless respects the boy's freedom and allows him to 'seek his fortune' by asserting

independence of law and custom in order to emigrate. The father evidently anticipates what will happen but waits – with great longing, one surmises, from the alertness with which he sees him even from a long way off and runs toward him when he returns. Meanwhile, no one needs to upbraid the son and tell him how alienated he is. He knows that from the way his life is falling apart; he experiences not only hunger and material deprivation but the degradation of a Jew employed as a swineherd (pigs being unclean according to the law) and the meaninglessness of the life to which he has been reduced. The story has him 'coming to himself' or 'coming to his senses', a Hebrew expression for repentance. Coming to himself, his impulse is to return, to retrace his steps, to go home to his father.

The repentance and the returning in this story do not seem to refer to particular transgressions, but to the basic condition of being away from the father's house in a false assertion of independence. What he repents is not so much an act or even a series of acts as a condition, a state of affairs, an outlook on life, a total personal orientation. The question as to his degree of personal culpability is not even raised, much less any question of having to itemise his unlawful acts during his absence. His father cuts him off in his attempt to confess his sin, because it is his mere return that makes the father's reconciling love effective.

The second part of this story is also a story of sinfulness encountering the reconciling love of the father. The elder son is to all appearances living in the father's house in willing dependence on him, attending his wishes. Yet the scandal taken at the father's inexhaustible compassion is, so to speak, diagnostic of the real personal orientation which is one of self-righteousness. In a sense, he is asserting as much illegitimate independence as the younger son, but more subtly. The father speaks to him with the same compassion and love but he is not able to perceive that. There is a sense in which, contrary to appearances, he is not living in the father's house nor attuned to the father's will. In fact, he finds the father's judgement flawed and his outlook unfair and ridiculous. He is as alienated as his brother but is unable to see that.
Sign of Reconciliation & Conversion

Exercise

1. The story of the Prodigal Son presents the younger son as the one who has sought false independence from his father and has thus become alienated. In what ways do we have similar experiences today?

2. Contemplate times when you may have 'come to your senses'. Trace the steps that are involved in this process.

3. The elder son is presented as one who 'is as alienated as his brother but is unable to see that'. Explain how this is so.

The Sacrament of Reconciliation

A BRIEF HISTORY

1. ## New Testament times
   The basic call of Jesus in the New Testament is the call to conversion to a way of life that is centred on God. Baptism was the primary way in which a person declared his or her adoption of a new way of life. When a person was baptised he or she left behind one way of life for another. There was a very real turning to God. However, in time, the question arose as to what would happen to someone who had sinned against God and the community after receiving Baptism. In Paul's letter to the Corinthians we find a reference to excommunication for one who has caused scandal to the community (1 Co 5:1-5). In the second letter to the Corinthians we find a description of reconciliation with the community that is available to those whose offence was serious enough to cause grave difficulties for the community. The big factor for the New Testament Church was that it was a community of love and did not want its members bringing that reputation into disrepute.

2. ## The early Church (100-400 AD)
   Venial or less serious sin did not cause so much difficulty for the early Church. It could be forgiven through prayer, good works and the Eucharist, especially with the recitation of the Lord's Prayer. The main difficulty for the early Church was what was to be done with a person who had committed serious or mortal sin. To be forgiven the sinner had to enter into an order known as *penitents*. He or she confessed the sin to the bishop and this confession was followed by a period of public penance which could last for many years. The penitent not only had to wear sackcloth and ashes but also had to fast and abstain and even refrain from marital relations. Eventually the person was reconciled to the community but had to be sponsored again by a fellow Christian, as happened at Baptism. This reconciliation was almost like a second Baptism and, since it could only be administered once in a person's life, and since the penance involved was so severe, people delayed reception of this experience of this sacrament until they were close to death.

   The main strength of this experience of the Sacrament of Penance was that it emphasised the community as part of Christian living and the impact that sin had on this community. However, it was harsh on the individual.

3. ## The Middle Ages (500-1100 AD)
   The practice of individual private confession began in the sixth century with the Irish monks. As the monks tried to live the Christian life, they sought guidance from an older, trusted, holy man – a kind of spiritual father. Such a man became one's *anamchara* – the friend of one's soul. A monk would not only confess his sins to such a man, but would also share his thoughts, feelings and hopes, indeed his inner desires and secrets. The anamchara served as a guide, not only because he was older (not every older monk was considered suitable to be a spiritual father), but because he had also trodden that journey and so could both share and serve as a model for the other monk. Something of this idea

is captured by Alastair Campbell when he talks about the role of such a caring person today:

> Because he or she has known within self the sense of failure and lostness which the other feels, the steadfastness and wholeness offered is grounded in human reality…. If I can find some courage, hope and transcendence in the midst of life, then I can help my fellow men find that same wholeness; for I know that I am no better than they, no wiser, no more deserving of such fulfilment.
> *Rediscovering Pastoral Care*

The elder monk not only heard the confessions of the monks in the monastery, he also absolved them. Gradually this practice spread around other monasteries and to Europe and also extended to lay people living around the monasteries.

Jerpoint Abbey, Co. Kilkenny, 12th century

The main strength of this experience of the Sacrament of Penance was that it was personal and focused on sin in the context of the overall direction of one's life rather than on sin as a list of offences. However, it did result in de-emphasising the community aspect of sin and forgiveness and so made reconciliation seem a somewhat private affair. The following chart highlights some of the differences between the practice of penance in the early Church and in the Middle Ages.

EARLY CHURCH	MIDDLE AGES
1. The emphasis was on public penance.	1. The emphasis was on private confession.
2. Confession was made to a bishop – usually only once in one's lifetime.	2. Confession was made to a priest as often as one wished.
3. Only serious sins were confessed.	3. All sins could be confessed.
4. Penance was public and carried out over a long period of time in the community.	4. Penance was given from a book, then carried out by the penitent.
5. Reconciliation, a 'second Baptism', took place in Holy Week.	5. The penitent returned for final absolution. Around 1000 AD absolution was given immediately after confession.

4. The Late Middle Ages (1100-1400 AD)
The Sacrament of Penance was defined by theologians. The mentality of this period was that before receiving communion a person should confess all his or her sins. The result was that people rarely received communion. The Fourth Lateran Council (1215) prescribed that people should receive communion at least once a year. Thus it taught that Catholics must confess their serious sins to a priest at least once a year.

5. The Council of Trent to modern times
The Council of Trent defined how private confession should take place. It also decreed that a grill or screen should separate the penitent from the priest. While this protected the anonymity of the sinner, it increased the individual and secret character of how the sacrament was now practised. This period also saw an increase in the frequency of confession. This was largely because the confession of even minor sins was seen as a prerequisite for the reception of Holy Communion.

6. The Sacrament of Reconciliation today
Today, the sacrament we have been discussing is described as the Sacrament of *Reconciliation*. In the early Church it was known as *Penance,* in later times *Confession.* Today the sacrament emphasises the need to be reconciled with God and with one's neighbour. Vatican II allows for three rites for the celebration of the sacrament:

1. Celebration for the individual penitent which emphasises the personal nature of one's relationship with God and the personal experience of sin, of conversion and of reconciliation. In this rite the priest represents not just the God of forgiveness but also the community. (To argue, 'Why can't I confess directly to God?' is to seek to deny the community aspect of sin.) Ideally, this rite should resemble the early experience of private confession in the monastic tradition where the monk was seen as one's spiritual director, one's *'anamchara'* – the friend of one's soul.

2. Communal celebration for several penitents with individual confession and absolution. It is usually celebrated at times like Christmas and Easter when the community gathers to prepare for these major events in the life of the Church. The rite usually includes the Liturgy of the Word, a call to conversion, an examination of conscience and individual confession and absolution. This rite emphasises the community aspect of sin and reconciliation while also helping to keep in mind social sin or the sin of the community in which each of us is involved and is therefore to some extent responsible for.

3. Communal celebration with general confession and absolution: this rite is reserved for emergency situations when there may not be enough time or enough priests to hear confessions individually. During this rite the participants confess their sins in a general way as a community and receive absolution together. However, when the emergency situation passes, these individuals should confess their sins to a priest individually.

Exercise
1. From your study of the history of the Sacrament of Reconciliation what aspects of the sacrament appeal to you most? Why?
2. Is the Sacrament of Reconciliation necessary today? Explain your answer.

CHAPTER 8

The Sacrament of Marriage

> This chapter presents the ideal that marriage proposes. Despite people's experience to the contrary such hopes and expectations of marriage still reside in the human heart. This chapter asks why. It also considers human sexuality and the nature of marriage.

Introduction

This poem, entitled 'A Marriage', was written by R. S. Thomas after the death of his wife:

> We met
>   under a shower
> of bird–notes.
>   Fifty years passed,
> love's moment
>   in a world in
> servitude to time.
>   She was young;
> I kissed with my eyes
>   closed and opened
> them on her wrinkles.
>   'Come' said death,
> choosing her as his
>   partner for
> the last dance. And she,
>   who in life
> had done everything
>   with a bird's grace,
> opened her bill now
>   for the shedding
> of one sigh no
>   heavier than a feather.

In *Man's Search for Meaning* the psychiatrist Victor Frankl, a survivor of the concentration camp at Auschwitz, wrote:

> We stumbled on in the darkness, over big stones and through large puddles, along the one road leading from the camp. The accompanying guards kept shouting at us and driving us with the butts of their rifles. Anyone with very sore feet supported himself on his neighbour's arm. Hardly a word was spoken; the icy wind did not encourage talk. Hiding his mouth behind his upturned collar, the man marching next to me whispered suddenly: 'If our wives could see us now! I do hope they are better off in their camps and don't know what is happening to us.' That brought thoughts of my own wife to mind.
>
> Occasionally I looked at the sky, where the stars were fading and the pink light of the morning was beginning to spread behind a dark bank of clouds. But my mind clung to my wife's image, imagining it with an uncanny acuteness.
>
> A thought transfixed me: for the first time in my life I saw the truth as it is set into song by so many poets, proclaimed as the final wisdom by so many thinkers. The truth – that love is the ultimate and the highest goal to which man can aspire. Then I grasped the meaning of the greatest secret that human poetry and human thought and belief have to impart: The salvation of man is through love and in love. I understood how a man who has nothing left in this world still may know bliss, be it only for a brief moment, in the contemplation of his beloved. In a position of utter desolation, when man cannot express himself in positive action, when his only achievement may consist in enduring his sufferings in the right way – an honourable way – in such a position man can, through loving contemplation of the image he carries of his beloved, achieve fulfilment. For the first time in my life I was able to understand the meaning of the words, 'The angels are lost in perpetual contemplation of an infinite glory'.
>
> In front of me a man stumbled and those following him fell on top of him. The guard rushed over and used his whip on them all. Thus my thoughts were interrupted for a few minutes. But soon my soul found its way back from the prisoner's existence to another world, and I resumed talk with my loved one: I asked her questions, and she answered; she questioned me in return, and I answered.
>
> 'Stop!' We had arrived at our work site. Everybody rushed into the dark hut in the hope of getting a fairly decent tool. Each prisoner got a spade or a pickaxe.
>
> My mind still clung to the image of my wife. A thought crossed my mind: I didn't even know if she were still alive. I knew only one thing – which I have learned well by now: Love goes very far beyond the physical person of the beloved. It finds its deepest meaning in his spiritual being, his inner self. Whether or not he is actually present, whether or not he is still alive at all, ceases somehow to be of importance.
>
> Had I known then that my wife was dead, I think that I would still have given myself, undisturbed by that knowledge, to the contemplation of her image, and that my mental conversation with her would have been just as vivid and just as satisfying. 'Set me like a seal upon thy heart, love is as strong as death.'

MARRIAGE AND THE LONGING FOR A SOULMATE

In each of these reflections we glimpse something of the ideal that marriage proposes, namely the love between a man and a woman that lasts up to and even hopes to survive death. Despite the fact of marital breakdown, we still find it difficult to dismiss the ideal presented here as unreal or impossible. Couples still hope on the day that they marry that they will be happy and fulfilled with each other forever.

Despite so many people's experience to the contrary, it is still difficult to erase that hope and expectation from people's minds. Why is this so? Why do people go into marriage with such expectations? What is it in human nature that draws them together with this deep-rooted hope? Down through the centuries, philosophers and poets, biblical writers and Church leaders have contemplated these questions. Plato offered this explanation:

> Man's original body having been thus cut in two, each lay yearning for the half from which it had been severed. When they met they threw their arms round one another and embraced, in their longing to grow together again, and they perished of hunger and general neglect of their concerns, because they would not do anything apart.
> *The Symposium*

W. B. Yeats wrote:
> I dream of a Ledaean body, bent
> Above a sinking fire, a tale that she
> Told, of a harsh reproof, or trivial event
> That changed some childish day to tragedy –
> Told, and it seemed that our two natures blent
> Into a sphere from youthful sympathy
> Or else, to alter Plato's parable,
> Into the yolk and white of the one shell.
> *Among School Children*

Something of the same idea is found in the Genesis story:
> Then the Lord God said, 'It is not good that the man should be alone; I will make him a helper fit for him'.... So the Lord God caused a deep sleep to fall upon the man, and while he slept took one of his ribs and closed up its place with flesh; and the rib which the Lord God had taken from the man he made into a woman and brought her to the man. Then the man said, 'This at last is bone of my bone and flesh of my flesh; she shall be called Woman because she was taken out of Man.' Gn 2:18. 21-23

The Irish Bishops' Pastoral Letter of 1985 echoed this same theme:
> There are few things in life more beautiful and more exalting than the experience of love between man and woman… each one singly would be so much less than half of what the two of them have become together.
> *Love is for Life*, 6

Exercise
Consider each of the sources presented here. What understanding of male-female attraction do they present?

Celebrating human sexuality

Our appreciation of human sexuality has had a somewhat chequered history. Today, in what is sometimes seen as the age of sexual liberation, there are many who recall, at times with humour and at other times with anger, some of the very negative attitudes towards sex in the past. Such attitudes were to be found not only in the Church but in society in general. In short, human sexual characteristics were viewed as being among those distasteful aspects of humanity's animal nature. Their only positive purpose was the propagation of the species. Those who were spiritually strong would resist such inclinations. Martin Luther, for instance, described marriage as 'a hospital for incurables which prevents its inmates from falling into graver sin'. (*Collected Works,* Vol. 44)

Such an attitude to sex resulted in ignorance, fear and guilt, as well as giving rise to the warnings, prohibitions and suppression of sexual joy espoused by many influences in society, including the Church.

Today we are much more aware of our sexuality. Many of the taboos of former times simply do not exist any more. Yet it is questionable whether in fact we understand or appreciate our sexuality any more than our predecessors did. In some respects we have as narrow a

Buddhist wedding ceremony

view of it as did those in the past of whom we are critical. Too often, in the name of liberalism, we reduce sexuality to physical acts rather than recognise it as

> a radiance pervading every human relationship, but assuming a particular intensity at certain points.
> *Nature, Man and Woman*, A. Watts

> The radiance of sexuality consists in the pleasurable awareness of possessing a body which is either male or female and the joyful recognition of the maleness or femaleness of others.
> *Rediscovering Pastoral Care*

One of the most beautiful celebrations of sexual awareness is to be found in the poetry of the Song of Songs which is, in fact, a hymn in praise of human sexuality and love. The man first appreciates his beloved:

> Behold, you are beautiful, my love,
> behold, you are beautiful!
> Your eyes are doves behind your veil.
> Your hair is like a flock of goats,
> moving down the slopes of Gilead.
> Your teeth are like a flock of shorn ewes
> that have come up from the washing,
> all of which bear twins,
> and not one among them is bereaved.
> Your lips are like a scarlet thread,
> and your mouth is lovely.
> Your cheeks are like halves of a pomegranate
> behind your veil.
> Your neck is like the tower of David,
> built for an arsenal,
> whereon hang a thousand bucklers,
> all of them shields of warriors.
> Your two breasts are like two fawns,
> twins of a gazelle, that feed among the lilies.
> Until the day breathes and the shadows flee,
> I will hie me to the mountain of myrrh
> and the hill of frankincense.
> You are all fair, my love;
> there is no flaw in you.
> *Song of Songs 4:1–7*

He is answered by the woman:

> My beloved is all radiant and ruddy,
> distinguished among ten thousand.
> His head is the finest gold;
> his locks are wavy,
> black as a raven.
> His eyes are like doves beside springs of water,
> bathed in milk, fitly set.
> His cheeks are like beds of spices,
> yielding fragrance.
> His lips are lilies,
> distilling liquid myrrh.
> His arms are rounded gold,
> set with jewels.
> His body is ivory work,
> encrusted with sapphires.
> His legs are alabaster columns,
> set upon bases of gold.
> His appearance is like Lebanon,
> choice as the cedars.
> His speech is most sweet, and he is altogether desirable.
> This is my beloved and this is my friend,
> O daughters of Jerusalem.
> *Song of Songs 5:10–16*

The ease with which each acknowledges the beauty of the other suggests the feeling of security and trust between the man and woman. There is nothing ugly or sordid in their profession. Rather, as the Book of Genesis puts it:

> And the man and his wife were both naked, and were not ashamed. *Genesis 2:25*

It is only later, after they have tasted of the forbidden fruit and thus sinned, that they become conscious of their nakedness and try to cover it up.

Question
Why do you think Adam and Eve became conscious and ashamed of their nakedness after they had sinned?

Sex as language

Perhaps one of the greatest differences between the animal world of sex and the human experience of sexuality is that for human beings sex is a form of communication. It is the language of the body. It is not simply an instinct-driven urge, the purpose of which is to propagate the species. As human beings, we invest meaning in sexual expression. We link sexual expression with the relationship between two people. Ultimately we see love and its expression in sex as intimately connected. Thus, as the language of the body, the key question in a sexual relationship is 'what is being communicated?'

> In love hands don't take, grasp or hold. They caress. Caressing is the possibility of human hands to be tender. The careful touch of the hand makes for growth. Like a gardener who carefully touches the flowers to enable the light to shine through and stimulate growth, the hand of the lover allows for the full self-expression of the other. In love the mouth does not bite, devour or destroy. It kisses. A kiss is not to take in but to allow for the full and fearless surrender. In love the eyes don't trap the stranger's body through a sartrian keyhole, nor do they arouse shame by the feeling of being exposed as Noah felt when his son Ham looked at his naked body; but in love the eyes cover the other's body with the warm radiation of an admiring smile as an expression of tenderness.
> *Intimacy,* Henri Nouwen

We often perceive the Church's attitude towards sex as being negative. Yet the real moral question which the Church poses has to do with an understanding of the human person as made in the image of God. The underlying principle is that of *wholeness,* where the person is understood in terms of his or her totality – physical, psychological, emotional and spiritual. Accordingly, *all human behaviour has to engage and protect the whole person.* Thus,

> Sexual union says, 'I love you', in a very profound way. By sexual union, a man and woman say to each other: 'I love you. There is nobody else in all the world I love in the way I love you. I love you just for being you. I want you to become even more wonderful than you are. I want to share my life and my world with you. I want you to share your life and your world with me. I want us to build a new life together, a future together, which will be our future. I need you. I can't live without you. I need you to love me, and to love me not just now but always. I will never let you down or walk out on you. I will stay with you through thick and through thin. I will be responsible for you and I want you to be responsible for me, for us, no matter what happens.'
> *Love is for Life,* 9

What this means is that all human behaviour, including sexual behaviour, is about protecting the total person in ourselves and in others. *Thus the real moral question in all sexual behaviour is whether it involves the whole person.* The 'act of knowing' is one expression for sexual intercourse that is found in the Scriptures. This knowledge involves the whole person. When two people give to each other totally in sexual intercourse without being able to give to each other fully and totally with other aspects of their person, they are saying more with their bodies than they are in a position to say with the rest of their person. In this situation, the language of sex is communicating more than is meant. Therefore, there is a certain untruth in that which is being communicated.

> Sexual intercourse is the symbol of total mutual surrender and union between a man and a woman. The symbol states an untruth unless that man and woman are in fact committed to one another and united with one another within the security and fidelity of a life-long partnership.
> *Human Life is Sacred*, 94

The morality of sexual activity centres on the truth – the truth about our nature as human beings and the truth of what we communicate to one another.

Thus 'the trivialisation of our age is not that of sex but of persons.... We use others for our pleasure and neglect our responsibility towards them' (*Proposals for a New Sexual Ethic*, Jack Dominian). Such a practice ultimately has consequences for us. The real human search is the search for intimacy – the longing for the soul-mate whom Plato and Yeats talked about. Sometimes people confuse that need with sex. They feel that they can achieve such intimacy through physical sex alone, but intimacy

> ...is a complex phenomenon with both psychological and physical dimensions. It involves a loving sharing of one's being with another and openness to similar sharing by the other.... Although there is a universal need for intimacy, the enriching experience of intimacy can be elusive. People become lonely and embittered, couples separate and divorce – all because they are unable to experience intimacy or because they experience it in frustrating and disappointing ways.
> *World Synod of Bishops*, Cardinal Joseph Bernardin, 1980

Sex, love and marriage

In one of his poems, Philip Larkin describes a medieval tomb in Chichester Cathedral which has a carved representation of an Earl and Countess of Arundel who are buried there. It resembles a thousand other tombs in churches and graveyards across Europe – the earl is clad in armour, the countess wears the stiff pleats of the fashion of her day. There is only one small difference: in this case the earl has taken off one of his gloves and is holding his wife's hand in his. Larkin, pondering this tomb, concludes that:

> The stone fidelity
> They hardly meant has come to be
> Their final blazon, and to prove
> Our almost-instinct almost true:
> What will survive of us is love.

The idea of permanence has always attached itself to love. Why is this so? Why emphasise permanence when many people advocate the opposite? Once again our answer has less to do with Church rules and more to do with our understanding of the human person, and his or her basic needs. The British psychiatrist Jack Dominian talks about love in terms of sustaining,

The Arundel Tomb at Chichester Cathedral

healing and growth, and argues that permanency is essential if such things are to take place.

SUSTAINING

We enter into this world in a one to one relationship between ourselves and our mother and this one to one bond or attachment remains fundamental to all our subsequent human experience. The first element of such experience is that of sustaining. We cannot survive our early years unless someone, usually our mother, provides us with material sustenance. The need to be provided for materially continues throughout life whenever our own ability to look after ourselves is temporarily or permanently impaired. With the rapid social changes affecting the status of women, their traditional economic dependence on men is diminishing and so is the need to please and placate through fear of economic damage. But there is of course more to sustaining than material welfare although clearly this comes first. There is emotional sustaining which basically means security. Security in turn means that we need to have meaning, recognition, acceptance and significance for another person who is in touch with our inner world through sensitive, empathetic communication and reacts to our needs with increasing accuracy. Reacting sensitively to our material and emotional sustaining needs does not mean necessarily eliminating them or providing all the answers. It does require however a minimum degree of permanency, continuity and predictability to allay our fears of abandonment, loss, repudiation and rejection.

HEALING

Beyond sustaining we reach a deeper layer of our being. If we feel sufficiently sustained, we show consciously or unconsciously to the person who is showing evidence of love the wounds we have accumulated up to that moment of time. These wounds are clamouring for healing; they are the wounds we have brought into the world through our genetic and constitutional make-up, and the wounds we have sustained in the course of our upbringing. Healing such personal wounds is a particular responsibility of the psychological sciences. It is the psychiatrist or the psychologist in special cases who will treat disorders of thought, mood, anxiety, the ability to relate at all or in a non-destructive manner which involves the familiar problems of excessive aggression, jealousy, envy and so on, but healing is not a prerogative of the behavioural sciences. We can all act as agents of healing by giving each other new healing experiences, providing the missing elements of security, trust, encouragement or whatever is needed and removing the threats of insecurity, deprivation etc. The great discovery of Freud through psychoanalysis was that the therapist can provide a second chance in life, a second opportunity to correct some of the experiences that went wrong the first time round in our childhood. Provided there is a relationship of love in and through sustaining, we can reach a bit further and deeper and become agents of healing towards each other. It hardly needs saying that healing cannot easily occur under circumstances of transient relationships. If we are going to take the risk of exposing our painful wounds, we need to trust the other sufficiently to feel that he or she can take our pain and handle it with care and effectiveness. This needs time, continuity, reliability and predictability. The essentials of healing do not occur in transient relationships although something good and precious can be bestowed in a transient relationship. But there is a world of difference between experiencing something good and entering into a relationship which gradually transforms our deepest wounds, healing the whole person.

GROWTH

Without the presence of sustaining or healing, personal growth faces enormous difficulties. Briefly, when we refer to growth we mean the obvious physical, intellectual or social growth that characterises the first two decades of life. This is self evident, but there is also the far harder concept of psychological maturation, achieving wholeness which plays such an important role in Jungian psychology. This growth means the transformation of physical prowess to athletic excellence, of intelligence to wisdom, of feelings and emotions to sensitive awareness and generous empathetic response. In brief, growth implies availability and realisation of potential. Availability means physical, psychological and intellectual access to oneself in an affirmative manner and hence to others. It is another expression of the dictum of loving one's neighbour as oneself.

It is essential to note that for growth we need not only ourselves but others because growth occurs in relationships. The most advantageous growth occurs within relationships which are not overwhelmed either by the need for survival, that is to say sustaining has been met minimally, or in which our wounds are not so obtrusive that most of our energy is taken up in coping with the attendant problems. Once again the most conducive conditions for growth are relationships of permanency, continuity, reliability and predictability which allow the partners to understand one another and to act as facilitating agents, bringing to the fore the other's hidden talents and helping to formulate clearly that which is latent and confused within; each acting, in other words, as midwives to the other by rendering conscious the unconscious, confirming talent in place of doubt and uncertainty, reinforcing initiative, encouraging experimentation, providing succour at times of pain, failure and despair, helping us to face and integrate the dark side of ourselves.

This is not to say that we cannot learn things from others or they from us in transient relationships but it does mean that the more enduring and widespread growth occurs within relationships that allow a reciprocal revelation of the widest possible range of our inner world.
Proposals for a New Sexual Ethic

Dominian argues that permanency, continuity and predictability are essential if healing, sustaining and growth are to develop. In this sense, marriage offers the kind of relationship in which this description of love can best take place. Thus, premarital sex and extramarital sex are not just illicit sexual acts of pleasure but are 'threats to those conditions which are the best enablers for the provision of love', and, therefore, for human happiness. It is this which makes them wrong.

The Sacrament of Marriage

1. Marriage in Scripture: The sacrament of God's love

Has it ever struck you as surprising that Jesus chose a wedding reception for the first revelation of who he really is? John recalls that it was at the wedding at Cana in Galilee that Jesus performed the first of his signs (John 2:11).

Yet, what would be a more natural place for Christ to start his work of helping us to grasp the depth of God's love for us? Throughout the Scriptures the love of man and woman is recognised as the richest human sign of the love God has for us. God's loving presence in human life is made known and shared in a privileged way in marital love.

When God decided on the most suitable image of himself for his newly created world, he created a couple, a man and a woman. 'God created man in his image… male and female he created them' (*Gn 1:27*). Both creation stories in Genesis culminate in the creation of man and woman who are so united that 'the two of them become one body' (*Gn 2:24*). Together they are to mirror forth the creative, fruitful love of God as they raise families and gradually make the world a better place for their children (Gn 1:28).

The last pages of the Bible echo the theme of these first pages. The Book of Revelation (Apocalypse) describes the final, full union of God and his people in the heavenly Jerusalem as a wedding feast at which Christ is the bridegroom (Rv 21:9; 22:17). Between these opening and closing passages of Scripture almost every book of the Bible looks to the marriage bond, with its joys and sorrows, as the place to learn the deepest meaning of life with God.

Through the experience of his own tragic marriage, the prophet Hosea discovered the mystery of God's love for his people. He describes this love not abstractly, but in moving poetry. He records God's initiative and his people's loving response: 'I will allure her… and speak to her heart…. On that day, says the Lord, she shall call me "my husband".' (*Ho 2:16-18*).

Isaiah states directly, 'He who has become your husband is your maker' (*Is 54:5*), and later adds more poetically, 'As a young man marries a virgin, your builder shall marry you; and as a bridegroom rejoices in his bride, so shall your God rejoice in you' (*Is 62:5*). Jeremiah draws on the language of romantic love in having God say to his people, 'With age-old love I have loved you' (*Jr 31:3*).

Jesus and his apostles knew these passages well. Jesus uses the same language, calling himself the bridegroom (Mk 2:19). He describes union with God as a wedding banquet (Mt 22:1–4; 25:1–13), and gives his body and blood as signs of the new and everlasting covenant of marriage bond between himself and his people (Mt 26:28).

St Paul distils the long Judaeo-Christian tradition in the famous passage in Ephesians (5:22–23) where he explicitly relates marriage to the mystery of Christ's love for his Church.

> It is not surprising then that it was at a wedding Jesus began the gradual revelation of his affection for man.
> *The Living Faith in a World of Change*, Carl J. Pfeifer SJ

2. The Rite of Marriage
   A short address by the priest

   I   Dear children of God, you have come to this church so that the Lord may seal your love in the presence of the priest and this community.

   Christian marriage is a sacred union which enriches natural love. It binds those who enter it to be faithful to each other for ever; it creates between them a bond that endures for life and cannot be broken; it demands that they love and honour each other (that they accept from God the children he may give them, and bring them up in his love)*. To help them in their marriage, the husband and wife receive the life-long grace of the sacrament.

   Is this your understanding of marriage?
   ℟ It is.

   II Dear children of God, you have come to this church so that the Lord may seal your love in the presence of the priest and this community. Christ blesses this love. He has already consecrated you in baptism; now, by a special sacrament, he strengthens you to fulfil the duties of your married life.

   N. and N., you are about to celebrate this sacrament.
   Have you come here of your own free will and choice and without compulsion to marry each other?
   ℟ We have.

Will you love and honour each other in marriage all the days of your life?
℟ We will.

(Are you willing to accept with love the children God may send you, and bring them up in accordance with the law of Christ and his Church?
℟ We are.)*

*(*The words in brackets may be omitted*)

III   Dear children of God, you have come today to pledge your love before God and before the Church here present in the person of the priest, your families and friends.

In becoming husband and wife you give yourselves to each other for life. You promise to be true and faithful, to support and cherish each other until death, so that your years together will be the living out in love of the pledge you now make. May your love for each other reflect the enduring love of Christ for his Church.

As you face the future together, keep in mind that the sacrament of marriage unites you with Christ, and brings you, through the years, the grace and blessing of God our Father. Marriage is from God: he alone can give you the happiness which goes beyond human expectation, and which grows deeper through the difficulties and struggles of life.

Put your trust in God as you set out together in life. Make your home a centre of Christian family life. (In this you will bequeath to your children a heritage more lasting than temporal wealth.)

The Christian home makes Christ and his Church present in the world of everyday things. May all who enter your home find there the presence of the Lord; for he has said: 'Where two or three are gathered together in my name there am I in the midst of them.'

Now, as you are about to exchange your marriage vows, the Church wishes to be assured that you appreciate the meaning of what you do, and so I ask you:

Have you come here of your own free will and choice and without compulsion to marry each other?
℟ We have.

Will you love and honour each other in marriage all the days of your life?
℟ We will.

(Are you willing to accept with love the children God may send you, and bring them up in accordance with the law of Christ and his Church?
℟ We are.)

Declaration of Consent
    P: I invite you then to declare before God and his Church your consent to become husband and wife.
I   G: N., do you consent to be my wife?
    B: I do. Do you, N., consent to be my husband?

G: I do.
   I take you as my wife,
   and I give myself to you as your husband –
B: I take you as my husband,
   and I give myself to you as your wife –

Joining hands, they say together:
   to love each other truly
   for better, for worse,
   for richer, for poorer,
   in sickness and in health,
   till death do us part
   (*or* all the days of our life).

II G: I, N., take you, N. as my wife,
    for better, for worse,
    for richer, for poorer,
    in sickness and in health,
    till death do us part
    (*or* all the days of our life).

   B: I, N., take you, N. as my husband,
    for better, for worse,
    for richer, for poorer,
    in sickness and in health,
    till death do us part.
    (*or* all the days of our life).

III P: N., do you take N. as your wife,
    for better, for worse,
    for richer, for poorer,
    in sickness and in health,
    till death do you part?
    (*or* all the days of your life?)
   G: I do.

   P: N., do you take N. as your husband,
    for better, for worse,
    for richer, for poorer,
    in sickness and in health,
    till death do you part?
    (*or* all the days of your life?)
   B: I do.

   P: What God joins together,
    man must not separate.

    May the Lord confirm the consent that you have given, and enrich you with his blessings.

IV   G: N., do you consent to be my wife?
       B: I do. N., do you consent to be my husband?
       G: I do.

They join hands and say together:
    We take each other as husband and wife
    and promise to love each other truly
    for better, for worse,
    for richer, for poorer,
    in sickness and in health,
    till death do us part.
    (*or* all the days of our life.)

    P: The Lord has joined you together. May he fulfil his blessing in you; may he keep you in his love.

Blessing of Rings

I   P: May the Lord bless ✠ this ring (these rings) which will be the sign of your love and fidelity.
    ℞ Amen.

II   P: Lord, bless ✠ N. and N. and consecrate their married life.
    May this ring (these rings) be a symbol of their faith in each other,
    and a reminder of their love. Through Christ our Lord.
    ℞ Amen.

III   P: Lord, bless ✠ these rings.
    Grant that those who wear them
    may always be faithful to each other.
    May they do your will
    and live in peace with you in mutual love.
    Through Christ our Lord.
    ℞ Amen.

IV   P: Almighty God, bless this ring (these rings), ✠
    symbol(s) of faithfulness and unbroken love.
    May N. and N. always be true to each other,
    may they be one in heart and mind,
    may they be united in love forever,
    through Christ our Lord.
    ℞ Amen.

Each places the ring on the other's ring finger. They may say:
    N., wear this ring as a sign of our faithful love.
    (*or* N., wear this ring as a sign of our love and fidelity.)
    In the name of the Father, and of the Son, and of the Holy Spirit.

The bride and groom exchange small symbolic gifts, saying:
    I give you this gift,
    a token of all I possess.

Nuptial Blessing
After the 'Our Father' four different prayers are offered to choose from.
I   Let us ask God to bless N. and N., now married in Christ,
    and unite them in his love,
    (through the sacrament of his body and blood).
All pray silently for a short while.

God our Father, creator of the universe,
you made man and woman in your own likeness,
and blessed their union.
We humbly pray to you for this bridegroom and bride,
today united in the sacrament of marriage.
May your blessing come upon them.
May they find happiness in their love for each other,
(be blessed in their children)
and enrich the life of the Church.

May they praise you in their days of happiness,
and turn to you in times of sorrow.
May they know the joy of your help in their work,
and the strength of your presence in their need.
May they worship you with the Church and be your witnesses in the world.
May old age come to them in the company of their friends,
and may they reach at last the kingdom of heaven.
We ask this through Christ our Lord.
R/   Amen.

II Let us ask God to bless N. and N., now married in Christ,
    and unite them in his love
    (through the sacrament of his body and blood).
All pray silently for a short while.

Father, you created the universe
and made man and woman in your own likeness.
You gave woman as companion to man
so that they should no longer be two, but one flesh,
teaching us that those you have so united may never be separated.

Father, you have sanctified marriage in a mystery so holy
that it is a sign of the union of Christ and the Church.
Look with love upon N., as she asks your blessing.
May she live in peace with you
and follow the example of those women
whose lives are praised in the scriptures.
May N. place his trust in her and see her as his companion.
May he always honour her
and love her as Christ loves the Church.
Father, keep this husband and wife strong in faith
and true to your commandments.

May they be faithful to each other,
examples of Christian living, and witnesses of Christ.
(Bless them with children and help them to be good parents.)
And, after a long and happy life together,
may they enjoy the company of your saints in heaven.
We ask this through Christ our Lord.
℟ Amen.

III Let us pray to the Lord for N. and N.,
who as they begin their married life
come to God's altar to deepen their love
(by sharing in the body and blood of Christ).
All pray silently for a short while.

Father, you created man and woman in your own image
and united them in body and heart
so that they might fulfil your plan for the world.

To reveal your loving design,
you made the union of man and wife
a sign of the covenant between you and your people;
through the sacrament of marriage you perfect this union,
and make it now a sign of Christ's love for his bride the Church.

Lord, bless this husband and wife and protect them.
Grant that as they live this sacrament
they may learn to share with each other the gifts of your love.
May they become one in heart and mind
as witnesses to your presence in their marriage.
(Bless them with children
who will be formed by the Gospel and have a place in your family in heaven.)

May N. be a good wife (and mother),
caring for her home,
faithful to her husband,
generous and kind.

May N. be a good husband (and a devoted father),
gentle and strong,
faithful to his wife,
and a careful provider for his household.
Father, grant that, as they now come as man and wife to your altar,
they may one day share your feast in heaven.
We ask this through Christ our Lord.
℟ Amen.

IV We call God our Father. Let each of us now ask him, in silence,
to bless these his children as they begin their married life.
All pray silently for a short while.

Father, from you every family in heaven and on earth
takes its name.
You made us.
You made all that exists.
You made man and woman like yourself in their power to know and love.
You call them to share life with each other, saying 'It is not
good for man to be alone'.
(You bless them with children to give new life to your people,
telling them: 'Increase and multiply, and fill the earth.')

We call to mind the fruitful companionship of Abraham,
our father in faith, and his wife Sarah.
We remember how your guiding hand brought Rebecca
and Isaac together,
and how through the lives of Jacob and Rachel you
prepared the way for your kingdom.

Father, you take delight in the love of husband and wife,
that love which hopes and shares, heals and forgives.

We ask you to bless N. and N. as they set out
on their new life.
Fill their hearts with your holy spirit, the Spirit of
understanding, joy, fortitude and peace.
Strengthen them to do your will, and in the trials of life to
bear the cross with Christ.
May they praise you during the bright days, and call on
you in times of trouble.
(May their children bring them your blessing, and give
glory to your name.)
Let their love be strong as death,
a fire that floods cannot drown,
a jewel beyond all price.
May their life together give witness to their faith in Christ.
May they see long and happy days,
and be united forever in the kingdom of your glory.

We ask this through Christ our Lord.
℟ Amen.

Exercise: Group Work
Consider the marriage ceremony under the following headings:
1. The Ceremony of Consent
2. The Declaration of Consent
3. The Blessing of the Rings
4. The Nuptial Blessing

What understanding of Christian marriage is revealed in each of these aspects of the ceremony?

CHAPTER 9

Reason to Believe

Introduction

Karl Rahner was one of the greatest theologians of this century. He was born in 1904 in Germany and was ordained a Jesuit priest in 1932. From then until his death in 1984 he was to publish over three thousand pieces of theological work. His unique perceptions and insight have had enormous influence on the Church's understanding of itself and on the whole question of faith. In an interview towards the end of his life, Rahner was pushed to answer why he still believed in God despite the many intellectual difficulties people have with faith today. He answered:

> Listen, I don't believe in God because I have worked everything out to the satisfaction of my mind. I continue to believe in God because I pray every day.

In *Free to Believe* the Irish Jesuit Michael Paul Gallagher considers three pathways to God – the hunger of the heart, the call of conscience and the wondering mind. In a fourth chapter entitled 'The Experience of Spirit' he writes:

> …there are moments when none of those ways seems to hold water, when a sceptical spirit reigns within me and the honest thing might be to declare myself an atheist once and for all. Or at least an agnostic. That point has never come and I don't believe it ever will. Why? Because of a fourth road that is both deep and mysterious, and hence difficult to put into words.… When faith seems in deep trouble for me on an intellectual level, or because of the sheer unreality of it all in today's world, or in terms of the exasperating warts of church-life, the rock that I fall back on lies within my own personal prayer experience. There have been moments of power, which I can neither deny nor explain, but which remain anchors of my faith. There have been times when unexpectedly the veil seemed to lift and I knew some overwhelming sense of God.… The sadness of life is that I have not lived faithful to those moments…

Perhaps we can recognise some of those moments in our own lives – moments when we became aware of something greater than ourselves – moments when we gained a keen insight into the mystery of life – moments that were triggered by an awareness of beauty, the experience of intimacy, or an awareness of the truth. Such a moment is described by Sean Dunne:

> One afternoon, when I was an eighteen-year-old student at University College, Cork, I stood in a shop in Shandon Street on the northside of Cork City, and this sense of other people's uniqueness struck me with a particular strength. I entered the shop to buy groceries. I stood at the counter, casually looking at the shopkeeper as he served other people. There was nothing special about the afternoon, the place, the people, or about my own state of mind. Yet, as I watched the shopkeeper, I had a sensation of seeing through him. I saw him as isolated from everyone around him but, with an intensity that frightened me, I also saw him with disturbing depth. He was no longer a mundane part of the afternoon. Instead, in his brown shop-coat and with his head bent as he totted up figures on the back of a white paper bag, he seemed to glow.
>
> In a world wary of transcendence and religious meaning, the language used to express such experiences has either been trivialised or deadened. This was the only time I experienced such an event and I am slow to make any claims for it. In some way that I could not fully fathom, I felt that what had occurred was a religious experience.
> *The Road to Silence*

For the most part we do not advert to these moments or allow them to linger. We are usually propelled along by some distraction. We may see that such moments are pointers towards what we might call the transcendent, but mostly we do not dwell on this. We let the moment pass. It is as if, in the words of T. S. Eliot, 'we had the experience, but missed the meaning'.

THE SPIRITUAL SEARCH – ONE MAN'S STORY

Throughout history, however, there have been people who were prompted by such experiences to go in search of the transcendent. Every culture has its stories of those who have embarked on this spiritual journey. In our own time, too, the distraction of superficial living in a materialistic world has not completely stifled the human need to take time out to discover something deeper. The attraction of places like Lough Derg, Croagh Patrick and Mount Melleray bears witness to this persistent human urge.

One such spiritual journey is described by Sean Dunne. His journey was recent, indeed ongoing, and to a great extent we share in the Irish Catholic background that was his.

Sean Dunne traces his spiritual odyssey in *The Road to Silence*, where he begins by talking about the religion of his childhood.

> At its most negative, this consisted of a morbid fear that punishment would ensue if I broke the rules of Catholicism.… In my childhood, every situation was permeated with rules and the main aim seemed to be to act in such a way that one would not be damned as a consequence of one's actions.

The Basilica at Lourdes

The religion of his childhood was also a religion of ceremony – his First Holy Communion, the Corpus Christi procession, the Stations of the Cross, the Easter Ceremonies.

After the age of sixteen, he lost all sense of Catholicism as a positive thing.

> To the disappointment and hurt of my family, I stopped going to Mass and instead walked around the streets of Waterford or strolled along quays where I stopped near chained railings and watched the Suir.

As an adolescent, Dunne found that his childhood beliefs, which were characterised by fear and guilt and the threat of hell, as well as a sense of ceremony and certainty, could no longer sustain him.

> The result was, at various times, an agnostic uncertainty, a void and, even, a mere going-through-the-motions of religious observance. Yet while I felt unable to practise the form of religion with which I was familiar, I was still left with a strong sense of spirituality. I found it impossible to believe in nothing or to believe that the world around me was a kind of cosmic fluke in which myself and others were merely accidents. I sensed the existence of another dimension and hovered between honest doubt and utter confusion.

The next few years were characterised by conflict and ambivalence.

> I found it impossible to take Catholicism seriously and to accept it totally.... Yet, with equal fervour, I found it impossible to let Catholicism go.... I desperately wanted to believe in something.... Without a religious belief or confident atheism, I felt adrift and afraid. To those who are never bothered by such problems or who are content with their own belief, this probably seems bizarre and absurd. Yet, for me it was vitally real. Catholicism had explained the purpose and meaning of life. If I rejected Catholicism, I was left to find another purpose and meaning.

It was the strong sense of spirituality that lingered in Dunne which prompted his journeys to the monastery at Mount Melleray and the Church of St Gervais in the centre of Paris, also run by a monastic community. It was there in the daily life of the monk's world of work, prayer and silence that, in the words of George Herbert, he experienced 'something understood'.

> For a moment, I felt that I knew what the whole thing was about and, deeply, I felt part of it. I had discovered once again that, despite all my arguments with the Catholic Church, there are signs of tremendous tenderness, excitement and promise. Some of them are social; some are liturgical; some are monastic. The best of them begin in an interior space that has been shaped by silence and prayer.

What brings someone like Sean Dunne to maintain such a spirituality and continually seek to feed it, while others are simply unmoved?

> Some of my friends and acquaintances had little or no time for religious ideas.

Why do some people experience a sense of God while others have no religious stirrings?

The American novelist Flannery O'Connor suggests that people have to be shocked into a sense of God, into the need for redemption:

> You have to make your vision apparent by shock – to the hard of hearing you shout, and for the almost-blind you draw large and startling figures.
> *A Good Man is Hard to Find and Other Stories*

Such a sentiment echoes the Gospel message: 'he has filled the hungry with good things, and the rich he has sent empty away' (*Luke 1:53*).

In other words, while people are seemingly secure and self-satisfied there is little room for God in their lives. They motor on, propped up by those things which give their lives meaning. Sometimes it is only in the face of death, or some other experience which removes such props and illusions that they begin to feel the need for God. In 'Batter My Heart' John Donne captures this sense of a kind of 'shock treatment' that is sometimes necessary to bring us close to God.

> Batter my heart, three-person'd God; for you
> As yet but knock; breathe, shine, and seek to mend;
> That I may rise, and stand, o'erthrow me, and bend
> Your force, to break, blow, burn, and make me new.
> I, like an usurp'd town, to another due,
> Labour to admit you, but O, to no end.
> Reason, your viceroy in me, me should defend,
> But is captived, and proves weak or untrue.
> Yet dearly I love you, and would be loved fain,
> But am betroth'd unto your enemy;
> Divorce me, untie, or break that knot again,
> Take me to you, imprison me, for I,
> Except you enthrall me, never shall be free,
> Nor ever chaste, except you ravish me.

On the other hand, the French philosopher and mystic Simone Weil became aware of the presence of God through a more gentle route. She had been repeating to herself George Herbert's poem 'Love', when the presence came.

Love bade me welcome: yet my soul drew back,
    Guiltie of dust and sinne.
But quick-ey'd Love, observing me grow slack
    From my first entrance in,
Drew nearer to me, sweetly questioning,
    If I lack'd any thing.

A guest, I answer'd, worthy to be here:
    Love said, You shall be he.
I the unkinde, ungratefull? Ah my deare,
    I cannot look on thee.
Love took my hand, and smiling did reply,
    Who made the eyes but I?

Truth Lord, but I have marr'd them: let my shame
    Go where it doth deserve.
And know you not, sayes Love, who bore the blame?
    My deare, then I will serve.
You must sit down, sayes Love, and taste my meat:
    So I did sit and eat.

    I used to think, I was merely reading it as a beautiful poem, but without my knowing it, the recitation had the virtue of a prayer.
    Waiting For God

FAITH AS SURRENDER

We are often uncomfortable with the word 'surrender'. It suggests giving in or being defeated. When this happens, we are no longer in control of the situation. We have yielded to someone else. So we become dependent on their mercy. We are particularly uncomfortable with this feeling as adults. Growing up has usually meant becoming independent and being in control. Yet we know from our experience that love is impossible without a certain surrender to another person. As long as we stay in control and keep up our defences there will always be a barrier to love.

> Love exists when you experience the existence of the other person as a confirmation of your own.... Faith, like hope, occupies a place of its own within the larger economy of love. Even if we give a purely secular interpretation to faith, we can distinguish two elements in it. The first and most basic of these is the willingness to open yourself up to another person or to place yourself in his hands. The second element is... you do not know how to justify the hazard of personal openness and vulnerability. If someone challenged you to show that you were justified in undertaking the risk, you could not do so.
> *Passion: An Essay on Personality*, Roberto Mangabeira Unger

Faith demands the same risk as love does. We will never work out an understanding of God to our full satisfaction. There comes a time when we either surrender to his gracious invitation or cease to believe. The choice is ultimately ours.

> I give you only one certainty:
> everything is uncertain. Joy and sorrow
> are swathed equally in my mist.
> Which of the two will your hand,
> groping forward, brush up against?
> Let this be a comfort (or a warning):
> no hold is firm; everything dissolves
> perpetually into something else.
> Here is my oracle about your fate
> as a man.
>
> Yet my breast
> is soft, and my embrace
> compelling, when I invite you
> to lose yourself in it,
> not knowing myself if you will find peace there
> or an endless fall.
>
> 'Cimmerian Sibyl', Margherita Guidaci